THE DAUGHTER OF AFRICA

CRIST SANTOSOL

Copyright © 2024 by Crist Santosol

ISBN: **979-8-9899507-1-3**

All rights reserved. No part of this book may be used or reproduced by any means, graphic, electronic, or mechanical, including photocopying, recording, taping, or by any information storage retrieval system, without the written permission of the publisher except in the case of brief quotations embodied in critical articles and reviews.

To all the children, victims of cultural abuse
and child exploitation around the world

Contents

Introduction 1
Dragons And Swords 5
Touareg 16
Safari 27
Black And White 32
Rapunzel 45
Chaman 49
Sacred Readings 54
The Red Light 60
Letters And Pistols 72
Paths Of Light 79
Wild 83
The Master Plan 93
The World of Ronald 107
New Life 117
Hell Angels 131
Pennysaver 137
Downhill 144
Bodyguard 155
Furious Rage 166
The New Era 172
Redemption 185
One More Time 190

Rectangular Memories 193
About The Author 231

Introduction

Through the following pages, the how's and whys of this story, stored in the memory and retina of our protagonist for many decades, will be unveiled from its beginnings. A revelation that may sensitize more than one person and, even more so, discomfort those who directly or indirectly participated in those events inherent to the imperfection of the human being and some misunderstood and corrupted minds. But let it be said once, these sensitivities will never be deeper and more pitiful than those experienced firsthand by Fabi, not in an imaginary story, but in real life.

Through many sessions, recordings, conversations, and painful confessions, little by little, but with patient ease, memories, words, and events were arranged, giving way to events never reported, which urgently needed to see the light.

Join me on this journey into my past, traversing some of the most unforgettable passages of my life, where the final destination is a place called "Forgiveness."

My name is Fabi, and this
is my story.

Dragons And Swords

Santiago, Chile. 2002.

Under the refuge of anyone's imagination, the halls and corridors of a hospital can be quiet and solemn, home to whispered conversations, voices that wander discreetly from one sliding door to another, respectful of the rest and pain of the patients. But the truth is, amidst the eternal hours of artificial lighting, smooth walls, white sheets, and gowns, a tremendously deafening and constant noise of alarms and intermittent electronic beeps exists. Swinging doors filter moans, hopes, fears, and ailments, like the fluctuating cry of a mother and the first cry of her baby, the groan of an emergency admission, or the display of a family waiting for good or bad news from the doctor peeking through the hallway—all in Dolby and stereo, with an echo, too.

It is a different world, usually the entrance and exit door of our lives. There is no social or economic divide, no titles, medals, accolades, hatred, or insults, nor the good or evil we have done during the journey. Money and Ferraris no longer matter, nor do stock market investments or beachfront homes. Here, we are all born fragile, naked, and equal, thus we depart as well. Here, the one we hated is forgiven, and it is commonly the place where we would give anything for one more day. The truth is, it is a place where sooner or later we all reunite, a starting point where, for many, the only thing that matters is improvement and getting out of there as soon as possible, before ending up in the morgue or being turned into ashes.

Even the most untouchable dictators find themselves here. Namely Augusto Pinochet Ugarte, who at that time had exchanged his medals and military insignia for an English tie gifted by his friend Margaret Thatcher. It was to be worn as a Senator of the Republic in the now newly born democratic nation, influenced by the "NO" campaign, finally fertilized by the voice of the people. And there, in that hospital, my mother, María Eugenia, was also present, holding her father's hand, the former Commander-in-Chief of the Chilean Army, my grandfather Sergio Castillo Aránguiz García Huidobro.

They were my grandfather's twilight hours, who suffered from lung cancer at the age of 90. Amidst the hypocritical silence that characterizes these buildings, and being the Military Hospital of Chile, symbolically, things had taken an unexpected turn when the sound of a cane hitting the floor reverberated, accompanying the unsteady steps of Pinochet as he entered the room. My dying grandfather, upon meeting my gaze, smiled and uttered his final words.

"Look at these two commanders-in-chief, what a state we found ourselves in!" he said to Pinochet Ugarte, laughter breaking out between the two retired military men and garnering the sympathy of Eugenia, who approached the elderly dictator to give him a cordial embrace.

Pinochet, smiling, looked at the woman and whispered, "And you, María Eugenia, are you going back to Africa?"

"No, General, I have returned to take care of my father, and this time I intend to stay in Santiago," she replied. "How is Mrs. Lucía doing?"

"She's doing well, my dear, a bit under the weather, but she is stronger than her father and me combined," he replied.

They laughed again and chatted for a while.

Pinochet knew him well. Sergio Castillo had been a distinguished and accomplished military man throughout his career, starting from his early years when he entered the Bernardo O'Higgins Military School in 1928 and graduated in 1930 as an Infantry Sublieutenant. He served as a Military Attaché in Brazil for a couple of years, participated in various military training programs in the United States alongside renowned American officers, and in 1968, he was appointed Commander-in-Chief during President Eduardo Frei Montalva's administration. The following year, he faced the military movement led by General Roberto Viaux, who protested and rebelled against the low salaries and poor conditions of the uniformed personnel in northern Chile, an event known as "El Tacnazo." After that serious institutional conflict, my grandfather resigned from the army for good. In 1973, his comrade from the military, who now shared the same hospital, was responsible for the death of President Salvador Allende, overthrowing the democratically elected government and taking control of the nation at gunpoint for over 17 years. Since that day, on October 15, 2002, after exchanging some memories and bidding farewell as soldiers, the comrades-in-arms would never see each other again.

Eugenia still held her father's hand, who in his horizontal state, gazed at the ceiling of the room and occasionally turned his head to meet his daughter's eyeline. A broken "forgive me, forgive me, my daughter" could be heard each time he did so. María Eugenia kissed him on the forehead and whispered softly, "There's nothing to forgive. What's done is done. Rest, Dad."

No tear rolled down her cheek for that exemplary soldier, for the man who raised his daughter amidst the privileges of the elite and the well-to-do society of Chile at that time, a country lacking justice, equity, and truth, but adorned with a notable identity characterized by empanadas, chicha, rodeos, kites, and cueca, the national dance.

María Eugenia Castillo García Huidobro. It's not like saying "I'm Mary" or "I'm John" simply, short and without embellishments like in the United States. In Chile, names carry social weight, and if they are long and pronounced with a bourgeois accent, as if wrapping your mouth around a hot potato, while meeting someone and giving them a kiss on the cheek, or both, it will be your introduction card that grants you stability, credibility, dignity, and honor within that compressed, relevant, and affluent social stratum. She belonged to that social class that appears in the press, on television, in showbiz, and in politics. She was a woman who grew up in a beautiful house, with a nanny included, a weekly gardener, rubber trees, and oriental banana trees, in an affluent neighborhood of the capital city. Important visitors came to her house, on the same level as the visitors to the military hospital, or perhaps slightly lower. Ambassadors, politicians, businessmen, military personnel, and influential artists from the polished and powerful right-wing were so common in her circles that asking them for an autograph would be seen as vulgar, but taking a Sunday photograph with them for the weekly magazine of the Santiago social scene was an honor and almost a tradition.

However, Eugenia perceived the world differently. That life seemed small, sad, monotonous, and above all, censored to her. Her younger sister, Patricia, was a woman more fitting to her social status, just like their mother, Teresa Paulina García Huidobro Eguiguren, a slim and refined lady who was also very reserved about her affairs. And for good reasons.

Among the three of them, protected by the privacy of the walls of their property, they formed a kind of mini domestic regiment where a life closely linked to military customs and traditions unfolded, including orders, schedules, and ranks of command. María Eugenia was treated like the "soldier son" of Sergio Aránguiz, a son who never saw the light of day. She was dressed and molded differently, less feminine, with more pants than dresses, with more toughness, more orders, and responsibilities, as if she were a rookie conscript from a rural region of the country, obedient and without rights. She was like a weary, rebellious, and lonely sailor in the middle of the southern Quiriquina Island, impatient to escape but surrounded by an infinite ocean.

Sergio looked at her with different eyes, and those eyes were not those of an exemplary or even blameless soldier. His wife, Teresa Paulina, always noticed it, but as a subordinate, she kept quiet and followed instructions. For their youngest daughter, Patricia, all of this was always normal, although this version of normal gradually turned into a bomb, a time bomb that would later inevitably detonate. Sergio Castillo and Teresa García Huidobro were my grandparents. Eugenia was my mother, and Patricia was my aunt.

In 1966, General Sergio Castillo was assigned to Brazil, so he, along with his wife, daughters, and Guillermina, the faithful and efficient nanny, moved to Rio de Janeiro. At that time, Brazil was an unstoppable developing power, a monster that was beginning to awaken and make itself heard worldwide. From being a country barely known for its agricultural and livestock production, as well as sugarcane, and from being a giant hacienda where remnants and ailments of black slavery by Portuguese landowners remained, it was becoming the new center of attention for the masses worldwide.

The responsible party is Edson Arantes do Nascimento. Better known as the king of soccer: Pelé.

Pelé awakened the South American monster through a "futebol" ball, leading the "green and yellow" nation to become world champions time and time again. From one moment to the next, everything began to gain fame as his quick legs crossed back and forth in the Maracaná, from the Christ the Redeemer statue, the Sugarloaf Mountain, the beaches, and the favelas to the explosions of joy, color, and exotic frenzy every February in the Sambódromo. In a national trance of happiness, cachaça, music, shiny and slippery buttocks, bright and sweaty legs, and tireless batucadas that, through their contagious rhythm, gave life to the samba schools parading one after another along the Marquês de Sapucaí Avenue. The Castillo García-Huidobro family arrived there. The lifelong nanny included Guillermina, who knew not only every corner, spider, patch of mold, ant, and occasional flea in the house but also the best-kept secrets within it.

In Brazil, it was impossible to hear a military march with Prussian reminiscences amid so much samba, carimbó, bossa nova, and the jolt of cultural change that the family experienced. The truth is, among the four, or rather five counting the nanny, my mother was the one who adapted the most to the country of "Order and Progress." She liked the black skin, African heritage, capoeira, and the Afro-Brazilian religious events. Previously, my mother had been studying in the United States, but she was never attracted to that country precisely because of its lack of cultural identity. In contrast, at age of 23, she discovered voodoo, cachaca, and macumba. And, of course, above all, samba, which suited her perfectly. Among the few things she loved and practiced, apart from playing her guitar, was dancing, and this dance was the exact therapy to help her disconnect from her own reality. By that time, my mother already spoke English and Spanish, and now, with her ability to learn languages, she was beginning to master Portuguese.

But after a couple of years, the samba ended, and the family had to return due to my father's new professional assignment in Santiago, Chile.

Back in their homeland, my mom took refuge in her guitar, and she had to go back to singing tonadas, boleros by Los Panchos, and cuecas by Los Huasos Quincheros and Clara Solovera at social gatherings when requested. So as to not forget and drown her sorrows, she would dance samba alone in her room behind closed doors. But at that point, Chile, the guitar, the family, she, and her secret no longer fit under the same roof. She wanted to run wherever, whenever, as far away as possible. She wanted to shout her truth to the world, but an entire army that could silence her in an instant. She wanted to shake off the sin, the unhappiness, and the helplessness of knowing in advance that no one would believe her. She was alone and lost, almost resigned to her fate. Her own mother, Teresa, bit her tongue in pain, twisted with shame, and hated herself for being cowardly and allowing the "what will people say" of the Chilean elite to be stronger than her honor and morality. If she could not speak up for her daughter, she would clearly be unable to defend her. I believe that fear was consuming my grandmother bit by bit, and for her, the word "truth" was like saying "execution." She had no choice but to fake smiles next to the uniform, swords, and medals.

My grandfather, Sergio, had a commanding presence, a broad yet intriguing smile, sharp eyes, and a dominant personality. He was a powerful man. So powerful that when Eugenia gathered her courage and confronted him, threatening to reveal the whole truth, he, with his typical confidence and sarcasm, offered to have her committed to a psychiatric hospital. He assured her that he could do it in the blink of an eye, before she could open her mouth. That's when my mother pulled out the ace up her sleeve and tremblingly shouted at him, from chin to knees:

"I have photos of your orgies with your military friends, and I'm going to make them public, you damn bastard!"

The General almost lost control, and for a second, his eyes nearly popped out after hearing what she had just said. But then, with frivolity and wise military tactics, he smirked mockingly and said:

"Who would believe a whore like you?"

Immediately after, as usual, and as he had done since she was a child, he grabbed her by the hair, dragged her into his office, and raped her again in front of the photos of O'Higgins, Carrera, and the founding fathers of the nation. When his personal war attack was over, he collapsed next to his daughter, sweaty, panting, and with barely enough strength to utter a word, he took her hand and whispered while staring fixedly at the ceiling:

"Eugenia, you're grown up now, you must give me grandchildren. You're going to get married, and I know the right man for you."

She remained silent. Then, with a tone between supplication and shame, she replied:

"Can I leave?"

"Permission granted," her father said.

After that event, it's impossible to say how many Guantanamo-style torture sessions my mother endured until General Castillo retrieved the photos, the roll, and the Kodak Instamatic that incriminated him.

My mother possessed an unusual beauty. Her height perfectly complemented her slender figure, upturned nose, and wide hips. Her expressive gypsy eyes became the focal point of her narcissistic attention when applying makeup. She gradually extended the black eyeliner on her upper eyelids. At first, it was just a few millimeters, resembling a lateral extension of her lashes. However, with the burdens of gender identity and the passing years, that line extended to surpass even Cleopatra's. It was as if it were a tattoo proclaiming, "I am a woman," contradicting the "tomboy" image that her father made her believe she was.

She was beautiful, young, and desired by the high society gentlemen of Chile. Her father, a man of his word, fulfilled his promise and arranged for her to marry a former officer of the US Air Force. Her husband-to-be was in Chile as a government representative for the Peace Corps, an international development assistance program created by President J.F. Kennedy. The man came from a wealthy and influential family, bearing the surname Zipperer. Describing him in detail is irrelevant because, by the end of this chapter, the new husband would have been forgotten. The point is that, in the blink of an eye, General Castillo orchestrated a wedding with a reception, hors d'oeuvres, a waltz, sword arches, ceremonial honors, and all the luxuries befitting his daughter's status.

When the moment came to hand his daughter over to the groom, Sergio and Eugenia exchanged glances. They silently conveyed a complicity that transcended words: "It's not about the future grandchildren but rather about ending this hypocritically, yet decently."

From that moment on, a monster awakened within my mother, much like Brazil during that era. However, this was a two-headed monster, forging a path through a swarm of hatred, fear, insecurities, disorders, panic, helplessness, and misery. It was a treacherous swarm circling and circling within a mentally abused ocean, where the person who should have done the opposite—loved and protected their daughter— inflicted such pain.

This two-headed dragon possessed two entirely distinct personalities that emanated from María Eugenia's body. One exuded charm, while the other spewed deadly fire. This monster sought to break free at any cost and by any means from its abusive master, and the new husband became the opportunity to access freedom and the keys to its cage: her own family home.

The first night that the newlywed husband intimately approached Eugenia felt like a mockery, enduring the weight, and panting once again from another soldier, whom she neither loved nor would ever love. Everything seemed so familiar, repeating itself, including the chair in the dimly lit room, upon which a military uniform like her father's, albeit bearing a different flag, lay. Zipperer did not realize how or when Eugenia slipped through his fingers. After just a few weeks, my mother took whatever she could carry in her hands and fled, crossing the border and evading immigration controls.

She returned to a place where no one would find her, where she had briefly been happy: Brazil. Zipperer made no effort to find her and, shortly after that, he annulled the marriage, abandoned Chile, and returned to Georgia to begin his career as a respected lawyer.

During that time, the spirit of anarchy and rebellion against the political statutes that sought to structure a pyramid-like power hierarchy, led by the United States and trickling down to a sorrowful second order consisting of Latin America and the rest of the world, was brewing through massive social upheavals and movements that championed peace and freedom above capitalist interests and senseless wars like the horrific Vietnam War. While Woodstock boasted a utopia of social liberation, saturated with daisy necklaces and flower crowns atop heads, with alcohol, marijuana, and open sexuality, the Black Panthers sought to eradicate racial segregation, and the Cubans struggled to endure the economic humiliation imposed by the northern country. The revolt was pervasive across the world. Each country tried to adjust with what it had and could muster against the empire that aggressively meddled in its internal affairs, all with a clear profit motive and exploitation of foreign resources. What else could be done but to sing, dance, and bang pots in protest against these global injustices?

With its copper, wood, and sea, Chile was not exempt from participating in these international adjustments orchestrated by Uncle Sam, the avaricious elderly man in red, white, and blue. It so happened that during that time, my mother wanted to escape from all the oppression. She was a radical, like all youth, wanting to uproot established norms and try something new. The youth of that era thrived on sensations, adventures, risks, passion, and impossible dreams. The only unreal things that existed back then were the pages of superhero comics. Everything else was experienced firsthand. That's why from music played an unprecedented role from the 1960s to the 1990s, brimming with creativity and genuine social expression, including the samba and the bossa.

In Brazil, my mother adapted quickly as she was already familiar with the language and because it was a society that helped her control her two-headed dragon, amplifying the gentle side and pacifying the fire-breathing monster. She started making a living as a tour guide, which suited the loving and sociable monster quite well.

She assimilated into the culture to such an extent that she moved with the batucada like a piston belongs and moves within an engine cylinder, making everything else move in unison. No one knew her true destiny; she was a refugee fleeing from a battlefield. A personal defense maneuver became her own revolution. Her settling of scores becoming her own protest.

Touareg

Four years before María Eugenia fled to Brazil, Sam, not the old greedy imperialist, but Samuel Armstrong, arrived in Chile on a flight from the United States. He was joined by his wife and a whole educational aid plan backed by UNESCO, the organization for which he worked as an Agricultural Engineer. Sam Armstrong already had a couple of notable curriculum proposals before working in this field, having been a pilot in the US Air Force during the Korean War in 1953, alongside his teaching experience and diplomas from Stanford. Some time ago, he had fallen in love and ended up marrying an Irish artistic painter named Judith, whose relationship lasted only a couple of years because shortly after setting foot in South America, she, still very young and confused (another radical of the time), decided to leave him because she needed time to reorganize her life and her feelings. A few months after her arrival, she left Sam with a broken heart in the land of copper minerals and extended cordillera.

But soon the man not only began to embrace his newfound singleness and the Spanish language but also got to know the land and the virtues of agriculture in the South American country, especially in winemaking, where his expertise surely contributed to producing some of the world's most acclaimed barrels of wine. Of German-Scottish descent, Samuel was a restless soul and a brilliant mind, always connected to nature and an animal lover. I am not sure how many lovers he had before the artist, but I do know that with his Kenny Rogers-like appearance and his deep belief in and practice of "freedom" in the

American style, was enough to attract both daring and cautious females who crossed his path. Despite these attributes, his adventurous spirit prevented him from establishing long-lasting relationships. Once he completed his mission in Chile, he packed his bags once again and set off for his new destination designated by UNESCO. Of all places, he was sent to somewhere we've been to before; Pele's home, Brazil.

In Rio de Janeiro, short sleeves, sandals, and informality prevail. People go to the office without ties or jackets. They have coffee at noon to match the outside temperature with their bodies. They play soccer barefoot, and at the end of the game, whether it's on the beach or in the neighborhoods, it never matters much which team wins. What matters is finishing with a smile, sharing mango or pineapple while the juice drips from the chins.

Ipanema and Copacabana are the icing on the cake for those who arrive and desire to be amazed by the urge to live and have a good time. There, surfers, bikinis, glistening bodies, bicycles, bathers, and merchants, their long curvaceous coastal promenade adorned with parallel waves of black and white mosaic tiles, with people coming and going, music, fruit, the sea, the sun, everything blends in flawless harmony. The perfect place to bring a tour guide and an agricultural engineer together, all distractions made secondary to the love that bound them after laying eyes on each other. It was there that they met, two adventurers hailing from the same country between the Andes and the Pacific. Two refugees, two liberal hippies tired of the pains and tribulations of the world and life.

February had arrived, and Sam couldn't miss what every Brazilian and tourist do in February in Rio de Janeiro: go to Carnival. Amidst the feathers and explosion of colors, the music at infinite decibels, and the "garotada," suddenly his eyes stopped darting around as his pupils focused like those of a nocturnal cat on this woman dancing almost naked with a wide, white smile. She had the look of a Spanish flamenco dancer, moving as if under a trance or ancient ritual, with her hips on the verge of dislocating, where the only thing that mattered in the world was sweating, singing, and laughing to the rhythm of the batucada. The adventurer followed her gaze until she disappeared into the crowd, never thinking that they're paths would cross again.

Samuel, the resourceful, intrepid, and nomadic man like the Touareg, the tribe that roams freely through the vast Sahara, paid for a tour to explore the city. Suddenly, like a rabbit from a magician's hat, there she was, that gypsy woman with a wide smile, who spoke English, Portuguese, and Spanish depending on who asked her questions. Perhaps due to the side effects of caipirinhas and beer, he wasn't sure if she was the same belly dancer who had shaken her hips a few nights before, but he didn't hesitate to dispel any doubts. He pretended to be very distracted taking photographs until everyone got off and moved away from the tourism bus, and then, with his air of an indifferent but hungry shark, he approached and asked her:

"Where are you from?"

And she, still unaware that he was the last passenger, adjusting her hair and the scarf around her neck, replied, "I am from Chile, but I moved here a while ago."

"Are you serious? I am from the United States, and I just arrived from Chile too! I was working down there for a couple of years."

"So, you speak Spanish?" María Eugenia responded, starting to feel curious about this worldly man, now adjusting her hair more for the sake of flirtation than keeping it in order.

"I can understand much more than what I speak, but you could help me practice more," he replied, his tongue coiled and lips barely opening, trailing off with a Hollywood cowboy smile. That was enough for María Eugenia to believe that her solitude in Brazil had its days numbered. Without realizing it, she began to melt under the charms of the gringo, and in turn, she revealed her ultra feminine side that had been repressed and abused for years.

In Copacabana, the sun rises from the sea but doesn't hide behind the horizon. Instead, it sets to the south, beside the Sugarloaf Mountain, turning the sunset into a very romantic backdrop, later adorned by the city lights reflecting on the entire bay. Extending an invitation to dinner in that atmosphere was a definite yes. Since that night, two brains and two hearts found each other to share in their dreams, their desires, their sorrows and stories, but above all, to continue discovering the world beyond, while Christ the Redeemer with his open arms said to them, "Go, go, revolutionary children of God," watching them from the peak of The Corcovado.

First, they both sent their divorce papers, Sam with the artist and Eugenia with the peace officer, although she never confessed to him that she had been previously married, and María Eugenia arranged the annulment secretly without raising any suspicion from Sam. Once the annulment process was completed, they got married, deeply in love. Through a discreet phone call, María Eugenia contacted her mother, Teresa Paulina, and secretly invited her to the ceremony. She was the only guest, and afterwards, she returned to Chile.

They worked hard and diligently to save money and plan everything. The only thing they didn't need to gather was their eagerness, which was abundant, along with the vitality of their youth. They boarded the plane with just a couple of suitcases and began crossing the Atlantic to reach Europe. France welcomed them with open arms, and their souls swelled with excitement as they stood together under the Eiffel Tower for the first time, their lips uniting in a kiss capable of dazzling the moonlight that peeked out just behind the structure. They stayed at a budget hotel to save money because they needed their own means of transportation. Two weeks later, they bought a green Volkswagen van, resembling the nature that Samuel Armstrong loved.

However, that wasn't enough for him. The minibus needed a more personal identity or accent. Samuel, a committed animal lover and vegetarian, painted an adorable little cow with a yellow flower in its mouth. The friendly animal felt free to happily graze on the green grass of the Volkswagen all throughout Europe.

It's said that it's not worth waiting 20, 30, or 40 years to regret not doing what you should have done 20, 30, or 40 years ago. What is worth it is daring to do it today and remembering it tomorrow. Following this, Eugenia and Sam felt an urgency to seize their youth and embark on an adventure, towards the unpredictable that lacked imposed responsibilities, regulated schedules, and established statutes. It was now or never. The feat of their lives was about to begin. The lovers didn't think for a second longer; they got in the little cow and set off.

The roads grew smaller in the face of Samuel and Eugenia's adventurous spirit, and the distances also shortened. Without realizing it, after two years, they traveled across France, Spain, Italy, and from Germany to Greece. Their adventures were an addictive drug of vitality that made them never want to end their journey. They would camp wherever they felt sleepy or wherever night fell, by a river, a lake, or near a hotel to take advantage of the hot showers. But after a while, the little cow started losing weight due to the lack of grass, and they had to stop being nomads and settle in France to generate resources not only to pay for alfalfa for the animal but also for their own clothing, housing, and food.

"We'll save money and change the Volkswagen's engine, and then I promise we will hit the road again. Maybe this time we'll go to Asia. Wouldn't you like that, my love?" said Samuel.

"Of course, Samuel, with you anywhere. We'll soon return to our nomadic life," replied Eugenia.

Samuel easily found people who needed his knowledge and experience, and he started working in what he knew best, in a country where the best perfumes, cheeses, and wines, like distant Chile, were cherished. On the other hand, my mother had many tricks up her sleeve. All she had to do was pick up the phone and unleash her loving monster, applying her pressuring influence, and using contacts that ordinary people only saw in magazines, novels, or dreams. She knew consuls, ambassadors, politicians, and businessmen scattered everywhere who would eventually secure her a relevant position in a corporation or company. Her anthropology studies in the United States could also come in handy at some point. She thought about working in a museum or university, but going from traveling the world to confining herself in a silent building required a bit more thought. Enclosed spaces didn't suit Eugenia well. She was one of those who needed space to breathe.

They rented an apartment from where, while sticking their heads out of the window and tilting them to the side, they could see the Eiffel Tower when it was clear. It stood with its blend of classical, Gothic, and Rococo architecture, doors and windows made of noble woods with hundreds of layers of paint that had formed a second skin over the years, cracking like porcelain. The walls were devoid of cracks, adorned with handles and hinges meticulously crafted from bronze through forging and hammering. The claw-foot tub, made of cast iron, added to the overall aesthetic, all working in perfect harmony. This orchestration aimed to accentuate Samuel's absence when he left for work, creating an atmosphere saturated with solitude and gloom that evoked a sense of nostalgia. It gave rise to a multitude of tragic thoughts, ensnaring Eugenia within the depths of the darkest shadows. In this realm, fear and self-doubt served as a potent alarm, rousing the dormant head of the dragon—the dangerous and uncontrollable entity that had lain still during their years of worldly travel. These involuntary flashes in her hippocampal brain would come, go, and come again, and the only thing that would pause them were sips of whiskey or the inhalation of cigarette smoke.

The strobe-like images inside her head projected the presence of her father in that room. Although she felt panicked at her inability to stop the sequence of images, it strangely evoked a macabre nostalgia within her. She looked at herself in the mirror and couldn't bear to witness her own misery. In those moments, the contours of her eyes would abruptly blur, and she would begin pulling her hair and slapping herself, acts that were in sync with what the General did in his afflicted mind. That's why Eugenia didn't want to be confined within four walls. She preferred being on four wheels, anesthetizing her memory with the landscape, the road, hunger, and borders.

Samuel had already noticed his wife's strange behaviors. Sometimes, after lovemaking in their bed, María Eugenia, perhaps due to the inherent pressure of the disorders she carried with her, would light a cigarette, and start confessing to her husband, unburdening herself of the weight of her past. It was as if these were therapeutic sessions with a lover who played the role of a psychologist. She would share details of her life, and he thought that listening and understanding her was beneficial, that these conversations were a good way to heal her trauma. Sam had never taken it too seriously, perhaps because it was difficult for him to conceive the stories his wife told, and he was incapable of bringing them into the real world. That was until one evening, after work, he found his wife drunk, lying in the kitchen with a cut on her wrist, bleeding out. Terrified, he did what he could to provide aid and ran desperately through the streets of Paris to reach the hospital with his beloved. It was then that he realized the conversations after lovemaking were not just emotional releases but the exhausting efforts of the other head of the dragon, the fiery one, the one tired of sleeping, being silent, and being censored by its gentle twin, urgently desiring to emerge into life and dominate the will of María Eugenia. She began to threaten him with suicide if he left her, and he swore that it would never happen.

One day he found her naked, crying on the staircase of the building, screaming obscenities out the window, dropping the empty whiskey glass. Another day he had to search for her in the neighborhood bars when she didn't come home. One rainy night, Samuel was delayed more than usual. He climbed the stairs, opened the door, and called out to his wife:

"I'm here, honey! Je suis arrivé!" But all he received in response was the dripping of the sink onto an unwashed pot in that chaotic kitchen.

After briefly searching the rooms, he tried to open the bathroom door, which was locked from the inside.

"Open up, Eugenia, open the door! María Eugenia, open for me. Are you there? Are you alright?"

The dripping onto the pots persisted in answering him from the kitchen. Then Samuel began to kick and pound on the door with such desperation that he didn't even realize when a large, sharp, painted splinter embedded itself in his wrist, causing intense pain and a serious injury. But the most painful sight was seeing his wife once again bleeding in the claw-footed tub with a couple of cuts on her forearm. Sam thought that perhaps all of this was happening because they had ceased to be the nomadic hippies who traveled the roads with the flowered cow, and that, in reality, they didn't need four walls that limited their lives, rather the four wheels of the Volkswagen bus that set them free.

Samuel pondered the matter and searched for the possibility of escaping Paris once and for all, to prevent this sedentary lifestyle from causing his wife any further depression. The arguments became increasingly futile and violent. Samuel Armstrong was a pacifist who, when he could, made donations to foundations like Greenpeace or

WWF (Worldwide Fund for Nature). He detested violence, so on one of those occasions when María Eugenia was sane but enraged and on the verge of exploding, she sent him to "go fry monkeys in Africa". Instead of engaging in the battle, he seized the momentum, quickly packed a suitcase with clothes, and fled to a run-down hotel in Paris. In those moments, he contemplated ending the relationship once and for all, but he gave himself a little more time to be sure of making a definitive decision. After a couple of weeks, when the waters of the Seine had calmed down, they started calling each other occasionally, but they didn't see each other for several months until New Year's Eve arrived.

There was no room for another soul on the Champs-Élysées, the city's most famous avenue, which dressed up to bid farewell to the year. The Eiffel Tower looked like a giant bottle of the finest French champagne that, upon uncorking, released its immense, noisy bubbles of a thousand colors, sounding like sizzling fried fish in a pan as they fell through the canopy. The air was filled with the scent of gunpowder from the fireworks, cheese, perfumed bodies, wine, cigarettes, grapes, oysters, and caviar. It was a masochistic balm for sensitive ears to hear the explosions in the sky and the mishmash of music from all styles coming from bars, vehicles, homes, and public speakers. The laughter, the screams, the applause, the kisses, all in a sensory spectacle that concluded at the illuminated Arc de Triomphe, an image difficult to forget until next year. That night, Samuel knocked on the door, and Eugenia, surprised, welcomed him by throwing herself into his arms. They didn't miss any party as they had their own on that night of "Le Réveillon de la Saint-Sylvestre."

They forgave each other and renewed the love that had united them. Through the apartment window, the lingering sounds of fireworks that didn't want to explode at midnight seeped in, and from below, with echoes between the buildings, there was laughter from people passing by the wet street, tired heels clicking on the concrete, emergency sirens, and taxis shuttling drunkards' home or to another party. The walls of the room had a life of their own, thanks to the colors of the night, and they provided a perfect setting for an intimate reunion between them. Everything smelled almost like the first time they saw each other stepping off the tour bus. Sam traced every millimeter of that long neck with his eyes, caressed Eugenia's back as if counting the bones of her spine, occasionally pausing to feel irregularities here and there of ancient scars she bore, yet discreetly he carried on, refraining from questioning, as his hands massaged María Eugenia's swaying hips and pearl-like breasts that, when illuminated by the lamppost's light, seemed to possess a radiance of their own. Out of the corner of her eye, she caught a glimpse of that soft and unblemished hand reaching towards her head, magically releasing her long, jet-black tresses. By that time, their clothes had become mere carpets, and her hair was the only thing covering her nudity. She kissed him with faint desperation, at times feeling the urge to push him away, but immediately clinging to him like iron to a magnet.

Eugenia made great efforts to control and conceal her internal struggles, making her husband believe that there was nothing else to worry about. She kept him captive and attentive to her sensuality and warmth, leading him like an entranced ascetic, succumbing to her manipulative gypsy charms. Afterwards, as usual, she lit a cigarette, and they discussed Samuel's plans for them to become a pair of Touareg nomads far away from Paris.

Whispering with an ironic accent into Eugenia's ear, he told her that he had already installed a new engine in the Kleinbus. She smiled, indulged him, rested her head on his chest, and they fell asleep as the city began to grow silent, except for the noise of a drunken man crying on the corner over a treacherous woman, vomiting everything he shouldn't have drunk.

That night, unbeknownst to them, I came into existence. Although, according to my father, it may have been inside the combi the following night during an impromptu escape to Cabourg Beach outside the city, when they set out to reinaugurate the green bus and their reconciliation. Nothing could have predicted that this reunion would solidify a relationship fractured by events as difficult to digest as my mother's suicide attempts and Sam's growing disillusionment with establishing common well-being. The truth is, my father couldn't bear it anymore, and that relationship was consuming his life. After a short period of time and having resumed meaningless arguments, they separated once again, and my father spent weeks sleeping in his Volkswagen wherever night fell on some dimly lit side street in Paris. Every two or three days, he would pay for a hotel to freshen up and maintain his cinematic beard, while every night, gazing at the stars, he would contemplate the melancholic solace of his solitude. The vinyl interior ceiling of the bus spun around as he contemplated finding solutions for both his personal and professional life. Three or four months passed when Eugenia contacted him and delivered the news: "I'm pregnant."

Both agreed that the forthcoming child could be the anchor that would stabilize their lives, the grounding wire for Eugenia's erratic behavior, and a compelling reason to move forward. For Sam, it was not only a great joy but also a responsibility that, due to his culture, education, and strong moral compass, he could not evade. For my mother, it was what she needed and what she sought to keep the cowboy by her side forever.

Safari

In the same way that no one can define, quantify, and measure the physical forces that bind the moon to the Earth, or the Earth to the Sun and the other planets in their perfect cosmic dance, and we content ourselves with simply defining it all as gravitational attraction. What happened to Sam could have been a kind of electro-mental attraction, sending electromagnetic waves that traversed distances, the roof of the van, walls, doors, desks, seas, and continents. And just as energy cannot be created nor destroyed, in his case it transformed into a telephone call originating from California, offering him a position as an advisor for the diversification of new crops driven by the Senegalese Government and the agricultural corporation called Bud Senegal. They were based in the United States, which included the large-scale development of pineapple, banana, and various vegetable crops. Samuel didn't think twice and accepted the offer. They sold everything except for their battered suitcases to take with them only what was necessary to their new destination. They left the van at a friend's house and set off once again, filled with hopes and dreams.

While I clung to my mother's belly, they pressed cheek to cheek, trying to share the small window of the airplane to gaze from above at this giant giraffe with a wide dress cooling off over the Atlantic. Dakar, Senegal, welcomed them, immediately making them imagine how long it would take them to walk hand in hand along the shortest beach because the longest ones would be endless.

The aluminum bird with the Air France logo rested on the tarmac, and the man from Massachusetts and the woman from Las Condes, Chile, peeked out for the first time at this land, both humid and dry, with shiny black skins and broad smiles as white as snow.

The first impression was the clean breeze and the smell of the sea. The second was the exaggeration of colors everywhere, as if intentionally the Senegalese did not want the beige color of the desert north of Africa to erase the greenness of the south, and in that transition, they never agreed on which color they would settle for and then each decided to wear whatever they pleased. The women, with slender bodies like Eugenia, draped themselves from head to toe in patterned fabrics of countless shapes and textures that became a clear example of how art and human imagination resemble the infinite. Noise, smells, flavors—everything dressed in some color.

It appeared that there was a deliberate planning or regulatory plan in the process of constructing the city, as the aerial view revealed symmetrical avenues, streets, houses, and buildings, parallel, well-organized neighborhoods. However, upon landing, it became apparent that there was a juxtaposition of what happened down on the ground, with taxis and motorcycles fortuitously crossing paths, just as a cyclist avoided a street vendor who alighted from a bus unable to move forward due to a woman crossing in front with her basket of baobab bread. Amidst this chaotic order, a dog, and a child crossed from opposite sides of the street, with a police officer witnessing the scene, seemingly an animated ornament invisible to passersby. It is like a basket full of colorful tangled balls of yarn, but as they pass through the repetitive dance of the knitting needles, they create a beautiful and flawless fabric that emerges effortlessly.

My mother fell in love at first sight. It's not that Senegal had something of Brazil, but rather, Brazil had much of these lands—something so native, authentic, and, although modern, also wild. They both found themselves in this world so different, with dialects that still survived from French, English, and progress, with customs passed down from generation to generation, seemingly intertwined in the very DNA of the people.

Eugenia and Samuel, each with their suitcases adorned with flight tags from around the world, stepped out of the taxi that stopped in front of the hotel. Their expressions had changed; they finally took a deep breath after feeling suffocated in Paris, and they celebrated with freshly brewed coffee at the café next to the hotel.

After a refreshing shower, Sam bid farewell to my mother and, with his German punctuality, made his way to Bud Senegal's main office. He would be warmly welcomed there by other UNESCO officials, all happy, as if he were a family member who had not had the time to come and say hello. Soon after, he would be invited to dine with his wife at the finest restaurant in the city when nightfall arrived. And the night did not take long to arrive. Oysters, fish, and various seafood adorned the table with elegant centerpiece candles and soft jazz playing in the background. Sam ordered salads, tofu, and lentils with mango sauce, while Eugenia delighted in her first glass of white wine in one hand and an oyster with cheese in the other. Many important people from the city arrived, and my mother, without hesitation, unleashed the chains of the charming dragon to work its magic. It only took a few words and gestures for the diners to understand that, she was the next in line after Queen Elizabeth. Her manners and grace captivated the Senegalese aristocracy, and from that very night, she had fans, followers, and saints in her court, especially because in Africa, things work just like in Chile—contacts, influence, money, corruption, names, and surnames. In Chile, they call it "chaqueteo", here in Dakar, something similar, but in Wolof. Suddenly, the jazz stopped, the lighting dimmed, the venue lit its torches, and the dance floor became a stage for drums with stretched hides and dancers painted and adorned with everything organic they could find to create a spectacle for the tourists, capable of awakening the dormant senses. My father and mother raised their glasses and laughed freely with the crowd of people in long tunics, with kind faces, people whose joy seemed to erase any memory of being victims of the Portuguese and English ambition with their slave chains during the 17th and 18th centuries. Sam and Eugenia watched with ecstasy in their eyes as those women, made of cocoa, with their lips painted black, earrings, and multicolored skirts, defied anyone who dared to think there was poverty there, with their pure gold necklaces and bracelets that seemed more like part of the percussion guiding the dancers and their euphoric movements than feminine jewelry. Eugenia was hypnotized watching the jumps and turns in the air of those perfect bodies, with chants that strangely differed, with harmonic scales distant from the typical treble clef on her guitar. They seemed like conversations where some would say something and others would respond.

In between, there were more voices and guttural noises, but she couldn't tell where they were coming from until she made eye contact and exchanged greetings with the three elderly individuals, with wrinkled skin and impeccably dressed in Muslim attire, sitting across from her on the other side of the salon. She thought that perhaps those voices were the ancestors of this people, who had also come to welcome them that night. Both believed they were happy, but compared to when they were pulled onto the dance floor, that was orgasmic joy.

Samuel, with his robotic American movements, doesn't deserve much description other than bursts of laughter and his long hair falling on his face and sticking to his sweat. As for Eugenia, she was reborn once again like an African phoenix, shedding all the baggage she still carried from the South American elite and surrendering herself to the rhythms of the djembes and the deep monotony of the koras. A beautiful dark-skinned woman with pearly teeth and rings of red and turquoise seeds in her braids approached her and tied a traditional scarf around her hair, immediately starting to teach her how to dance mbalax. It began with pushing the hips back and placing the hands on the open and rhythmic thighs, moving the eyes from side to side while shaking the tongue like Gene Simmons from Kiss. I'm sure that when my mother joined the dance with her exaggerated eyeliner, more than one diner believed that from the heart of North Africa, from sacred Egypt, the reincarnation of the queen of Alexandria, Cleopatra Philopator herself, was visiting them. The safari had begun.

The welcome party was unforgettable, and as dawn approached, the governor's elegant Mercedes Benz, with leopard skin upholstery, took María Eugenia and Sam to their hotel. It was Friday. On Saturday, they slept amidst the incessant noise of the ceiling fan with rattan blades and the constant buzzing of a fly that showed no signs of resting. Eugenia woke up a couple of times, her hand passing over the skin of her belly that protected me.

After a few weeks at the hotel, they rented a centrally located apartment, and soon after, the opportunity arose to buy a small house a few blocks from the beach. It was a humble, simple dwelling, neglected and eager for some "TLC (Tender Loving Care)" as Sam would say. But to begin with, it wasn't bad at all because it was a small palace where all of Sam and Eugenia's dreams and hopes fit, while also providing a large courtyard.

That was my cradle and my earliest childhood memories.

Black And White

On the 6th of October in 1972, my father took my mother to the Aristide Le Dantec Hospital Center, where, without major complications, I came to know them both for the first time. Eugenia was exhausted after childbirth, but she wanted to hold me in her arms as soon as possible to verify that this child, so fair and different from her own race, was truly her daughter. This noticeable difference in skin color aroused her curiosity, and she could affirm that the German and Scottish heritage in my cells dominated over the Spanish-Araucanian genetic legacy. I believe that was the day she loved me the most and fully accepted me, devoting herself wholeheartedly to nourishing me at her breast. On the other hand, Sam was the happiest man on Earth. Although his disbelief at seeing this child in his arms never ceased to linger, making it somewhat challenging for him, like many fathers, to believe that this fragile life, flesh of his flesh, had become a reality. Upon arriving at my new home, my father would spend hours gazing at me, contemplating me, while Eugenia took photographs of her bearded man and that defenseless little girl who bore no resemblance to her at all. With such fair skin, blonde hair, and green eyes, Eugenia had only seen such features in the logo of Gerber baby.

Sam wasted no time in writing to his entire family to inform them that he and Eugenia had welcomed a daughter. The happiest of them all was his Scottish immigrant father, who resided in New Hampshire and was thrilled at the prospect of meeting his new African granddaughter. On the other hand, Eugenia had no intentions of sharing the good news, despite her husband's insistence that she should write to Sergio, Teresa, and Patricia, using the news of my birth to reconcile their past differences. However, my mother's reluctance stemmed not from the tensions between her and the General, but rather from her deep-seated desire to escape him. When they lived in Paris, my mother told Sam many things that happened during her childhood and adolescence, but she hadn't yet told him about the sexual assaults committed by her progenitor, a matter that caused her great shame and humiliation. On the contrary, Samuel would never want his daughter near that monster. That's why when Samuel asked his wife, "Have you told your parents the news?" she simply ignored him or replied, "I'll do it, I'll do it."

On that occasion, when she was about to give birth, she confessed to my father that during a trip to Nigeria, she had been taken to meet and pay her respects to Ifa, who was the master and ruler of those lands, a holy and wise man, considered by many to be a direct descendant of Orunmila himself. He was a sanctimonious king who wore a long tunic and on his head, he wore his "fila," a very typical hat. Both were made of aso oke, intricately woven stitch by stitch by the hands of the country's finest textile artisans. His tunic had a V-shaped collar with gold-embroidered edges. The man never parted from his finely carved ebony staff, adorned with artistic details of its origin and lineage. Eugenia told him that on that occasion, the holy man rose from his throne, also covered in fine fabrics and impala hides, approached her, dipped a finger in a small bowl of oil of unknown origin, looked at her intently while drawing a circle on her forehead with the oily finger, and said:

"You will have a daughter, and you shall name her Fabi, for she will also be my daughter and the offspring of Orunmila. You shall call her that, and if you don't, you will not witness them grow," he said.

"Her name shall be Fabi, agreed, Sam?"

"I do appreciate the name, my dear, but let us prefix it with Andrea, signifying strength and bravery, qualities akin to mine. Andrea Fabi Armstrong how does that sound?" responded my father, a faint smile gracing his countenance, his hands damp with nervous anticipation of the impending childbirth.

Upon my birth, they took turns cradling me in their arms, their eyes filled with profound emotion as they gazed upon me. They were eager to acquaint themselves with their newborn child, ready to envelop me in their love and strive for the realization of an idyllic family. To commence this journey, my father conceived the notion of baptizing me according to Christian customs, despite his own agnostic inclinations. Eugenia, not particularly devout herself but hailing from a social milieu where interactions with priests of dubious vocations, yet formidable influence, were not uncommon, acquiesced to the proposal. Together, they embarked on preparations for my baptism. In Senegal, a predominantly Islamic nation, the existence of such ceremonies posed no challenge to other churches. It was a small and solemn ceremony, of which my father kept many photographs. In black and white, of course.

Soon, my mother would realize that an unfamiliar and indescribable force hindered her from experiencing complete happiness upon seeing me, let alone fully embracing the fact that she was now a mother, having brought forth a new life. She had multiplied her being in this creature, born not in the USA nor in Chile, but in the very land of Africa. Thus, the responsibility of changing diapers, feeding me, and lulling me to sleep, combined with these new four walls that enclosed her, ignited within Eugenia an urgent need to escape, to flee once again.

In order to fulfill her desires and, at the same time, meet the demands of motherhood, she urgently needed a job, or else she would become even more unhinged than she already was. Intrigued, drawn, and captivated by the African culture she had encountered, my mother pulled a few strings and used her important Senegalese contacts to secure a position as a Researcher in Human Sciences and Anthropology at IFAN, the French Institute of Black Africa. This position suited her adventurous soul perfectly, allowing her to pursue whatever would distance her from her own reality and the lingering memories of General Castillo.

Once we were well established, Eugenia hired a local woman to take care of me, to feed me and carry me in the traditional African way, using a large cloth called a kanga that acts as a kangaroo pouch, but is worn on the back and tied over the woman's chest. Of course, these kangas are available in millions of colors and designs. For Western culture, it may seem strange not to use a stroller with a sunshade, windows and mosquito net, brakes, cup holders, all-terrain wheels, padded handles for jogging, and a foldable seat for transportation, etc. However, for African women, the essential aspect is to have their hands free to perform all the other tasks that a woman with a modern stroller would not typically do, from sweeping and carrying water to cooking, always with the baby on their backs.

There were many more after that nanny who carried me during my first months. My mother treated them with the same military discipline with which she had raised me, making them work long hours and assigning them all the household tasks beyond their agreed-upon responsibility of caring for me. Many of those women ended up, through insults, cleaning or feeding the animals in the backyard with me in tow. Of course, for me, it was all a fun experience, especially because women often carry out their household chores while singing melodies that uplift their spirits and make the day shorter. I'm sure many of those songs were childlike and dedicated to keeping me entertained as I watched them from behind.

On many occasions, Mrs. Castillo would be absent for days on end, immersing herself in the wildest corners of the continent, leaping from tribe to tribe, documenting cultures, traditions, customs, art, language, and music for the anthropological institute where she worked. Gradually, she delved deep into ancestral rituals that had taken shape since the dawn of humanity, driven by her thirst for knowledge and understanding, yet also intertwined with the boundless imagination of Homo sapiens. In Africa, the primordial sun witnessed our upright posture and bipedal locomotion as we learned to do something different with our hands. Here, we learned to form communities and establish strong social bonds by collectively seeking explanations for the phenomena that govern life, through our vague and flawed interpretations devoid of science and common sense. From here, the first potions of medicine sprouted, the first unjust laws, the conflicting religions, and the eternal human ambition for power, often resulting in violent tendencies. For my mother, many of these ancient rituals and customs perfectly aligned with her afflicted mind, providing an outlet for hallucination, delusion, and reverie, soothing her fears and haunting memories.

During Eugenia's disappearances, ranging from Cameroon to Nigeria and from Ghana to Sierra Leone, Samuel would return from work solely focused on making me happy. Gradually ceasing to be happy himself. From a very young age, my father connected me with animals, and in that backyard, we began to raise a diverse array of creatures, nurturing my astonishment and affection for them as I grew. As I transport myself back in time, I can still see Ruby, my shiny black dog, and Baba, my little white lamb who would imitate my jumps as we played together.

Animals have a greater ability to recognize love rather than malice. In humans, it is well-known that when someone is born with a disability such as blindness, motor problems, deafness, autism, or other impairments, they often develop other abilities that transcend the common talent. It's as if the space that couldn't be filled within the confines of "normalcy" becomes saturated with art, music, science, or knowledge. In the case of animals, perhaps the limited neural substrates that produce consciousness and the perception of existence as an individual have given rise to the development of other senses that we may never be able to explain, comprehend, or even match. This sometimes makes me think that when we are children, we are much closer and more like animals, with a greater connection and common ground than adults, who are burdened with prejudices, perceptions, paradigms, and absurd mythologies. Animals are tremendously capable of sensing this divergence. And that could be seen in those rabbits that, instead of fleeing from a hunter's rifle or knife, found happiness and complete trust in playing among my small legs, just like that beautiful ram that approached to lick my face with great caution, making sure not to hit me with its thick, twisted horns. My eyes would light up at the sight of chickens scratching the earth or my cat nuzzling me with affectionate headbutts. There, Tom and Jerry or Coyote with Road Runner didn't exist. There was no distinction between animals and pets; for me, they were simply my friends. In that backyard, with its towering banana, mango, and papaya trees, and walls accentuated by damp mold and peeling paint where microscopic life expressed itself harmoniously, we were all equal. And beyond that backyard, we were still equal, even in our skin. I never experienced the concept of black or white. The darker skin tones were completely irrelevant to me, as inconsequential as hating the day and loving the night, or vice versa. Africa was my home, and even today, I struggle to understand the how's and whys of slavery. I am incapable of imagining my people running into the jungles to escape trained dogs hunting humans and young individuals being shackled by their necks, hands, and feet without having committed any crime other than being born with darker pigmentation in their skin, as natural as fertile soil mixed with water. It's like inspecting a tray of free-range chicken eggs: there are white, blue, cream, brown, speckled ones of different colors and sizes, but once you crack them open, they are all the same on the inside. I still struggle to understand why it took other humans as white as me over 400 years to accept that we carry the same multicolored hues of Mother Earth because we are made of her. My first steps were guided by those women with beautiful tones, cinnamon, chocolate, moist earth, mahogany, or midnight skin, not by an absence of color like black.

Despite my mother's strict command, some nannies arrived with their own children, who became my first friends, first laugh, the first fights and tantrums in symphony, the games, and the purest innocence alongside my animals. My father was a kind and affectionate man towards them, always ready to lighten their load. He earned the affection of the local people, and they often brought him gifts such as artwork, fabrics, vegetables, or fruits he had never seen in his career as an agronomist. But his moments of joy with the locals were often tainted by senseless arguments provoked by my mother's insecurity, in which, just like in Paris, she would threaten him again: "If you leave me, I'll kill myself, and it'll be your fault," "I'm sure you've been rolling around with the maid," "Don't you dare abandon me, or a curse will befall you." Immediately after, dressed authentically as Yoruba or Berber, her eyes wide, she would take the ostrich feather handle, take a sip of alcohol, and, with her Afro movements, begin to roam the house, spitting with the force of a fire extinguisher into every corner with her whiskey spray. By the time her eyes started to roll back, and she began to speak nonsense or sing in dialects, my father had already fled to seek refuge in a bar, on the beach, or in his office. She was the ultimate authority in that regiment composed of servants, animals, a bearded man, and children. Her threats were not with arrows, but with curses and "black magic".

When I was about two years old, my mother, tired of threatening my father with suicide, found a more subtle but no less cruel or shameful way to appease her untamable demons, and the gossip soon spread through the city streets. My father was leaving a work meeting at a well-known café one afternoon when a woman wearing sandals, with a child on her back, touched his arm:

"Mr. Armstrong, perhaps you don't remember me, but we have crossed paths near your house. With all due respect, I come to ask you to do something to stop your wife from having encounters with my husband. He is a good man and has a job that supports my family, please."

My father, bewildered but believing in the woman's distressing account, took her hands and assured her not to worry, that everything would be alright, and that he would take action. That time, like many others, since I was born, sitting in the courtyard alongside my animals, I listened to the screams, curses, and threats from Eugenia, accompanied by the sound of plates and objects defying gravity as they struck the interior walls of the house. Sam would emerge, drenched in sweat, clutching his head, gasping for air. Occasionally, he would approach me with a half-extended smile, taking me in his arms, silently conveying the same reassurance he gave to the unfortunate woman from the neighborhood: "Don't worry, everything will be fine." When the argument subsided, Samuel would take me to the beach, where he often photographed me playing with other children inside the pirogues, those long traditional fishing boats. Afterwards, he would grasp me with his large hands, swinging me above the foam and the ebb and flow of the waves.

Those were hot days, and I still recall the mosaic floor with its multitude of colors, devoid of any specific pattern or design, except for a dominant white that I would seek out along the edges where the shade provided respite, and the ground was refreshingly cool. Usually, the only garment they would dress me in was a cotton loincloth, nothing more. If there were any visitors, they would put me in a floral dress and tie two bows on either side of my head. Nevertheless, I remember being very happy during that time, and regardless of the arguments between them, it is the cherished memories of togetherness, lunches in the courtyard, and our travels throughout Africa, encountering kind people, savoring their meals, and inhaling the scents of the countryside, herbs, and oils that endure in my memory. My mother carried her camera with her wherever she went, and it was always a moment of smiles and laughter as we posed with Africans in front of the camera, especially when groups of children approached us.

Supposedly, whenever animals appeared, I was the first volunteer to pose alongside them. Sometimes, I try to imagine the sadness and stress my father must have felt. Questioning himself about why he was there, so far from his native Massachusetts, his friends, and his family. He found himself immersed in a culture and society so different, enduring the delusions of a woman with whom he initially had little in common, except for a shared desire for freedom and travel, which was enough for him to fall in love with her. I believe he was incapable of grasping that he was no longer as free as before because, apart from this wild gypsy woman, I had appeared without him realizing it, further limiting, and controlling his life.

He needed someone close and trustworthy to help him with his wife. He pondered over it and then wrote a letter to his mother-in-law, Teresa, to tell her about the struggles in his marriage, the increasingly uncontrollable state of his daughter, and to let her know that he had a beautiful granddaughter. Sam thought that perhaps all the stories Eugenia had told him were just part of her tormented personality, and he seriously began to doubt that the impeccable General had been responsible for all this misfortune. He wanted to surprise Eugenia, so in 1974, General Castillo and his wife Teresa Paulina arrived in Dakar for the first time. When Eugenia saw them enter through the courtyard, she burst into tears and ran to embrace them both. Her father, also very emotional, didn't waste any time letting go of his daughter's arms to reach for those of his granddaughter. He took me in his arms, and his happiness filled the air. He was balder and thinner, but strong, with his posture and his pleated khaki pants, reminiscent of General MacArthur, and his immaculate wide-collared white shirt. My grandmother looked at me with excitement and surprise, seeing the family's first "gringa" granddaughter. There were no reproaches or explanations, no apologies, or regrets. It was as if their history was forgotten entirely. Everything was perfect; we were the most perfect aristocratic family from Chile in the midst of Senegal.

They spent several weeks with us, exploring the country, meeting important people, relishing local dishes, taking photographs, and buying souvenirs and mementos to bring back to South America. Don Sergio was intrigued by a house on the outskirts of Dakar that was for sale. The house was large and had an enviable courtyard visible from the cast iron entrance gate. The property was protected by high walls surrounding its perimeter, with battlements resembling those of medieval castles, where archers once peered out with their arrows ablaze, cannons, or boiling water. The house was half-finished, with some walls missing and a neglected appearance, but it had great potential.

"Perhaps we could buy it, don't you think, Eugenia? How much do you think they're asking for it? The "castillo" of Castillos! Can you imagine?" her father said on their way back home.

A few days after their arrival, my mother dressed Sergio and Teresa in their respective bou bou, long traditional tunics typically made of Damascus cotton resembling Muslim attire for the pilgrimage to Hajj. This made them feel fresh, comfortable, and African. They returned to Chile delighted, and from then on, black and white photographs and letters went back and forth every month. After this brief period, the "ideal and happy family" disappeared because once my grandparents left, everything returned to that strange normalcy filled with senseless and unfortunate events. The best example being the day my father turned the corner in his Volkswagen Beetle and found himself forcefully pressing the brake pedal, mesmerized by the spectacle before him through the windshield:

María Eugenia carried me in her arms, completely naked, screaming curses at Sergio, at Teresa, at her husband, at the husband of this woman and that woman, and anyone who crossed her path. Sam got out of the car and snatched me from María Eugenia's arms, who didn't offer any resistance but dodged him as if he were invisible, continuing her delirious show unperturbed. He then left me inside the vehicle and caught up with her, embracing her and placing her in the front seat like a sack of potatoes. Eugenia and her dragons were completely unpredictable. One day, she would wander naked through the streets, and the next, she would transform into an anthropologist dedicated to rescuing and preserving everything that didn't catch the attention of the Africans but represented remnants of the dawn of humanity for the rest of the world. Every time she returned from her trips, she brought with her crafts, jewelry, pottery, musical instruments, textiles, masks, spears, leather, carpets, drums, and everything in between. I loved looking under the sun at the earrings and necklaces adorned with mother-of-pearl, gazing through amber and obsidian which created a shimmering and colorful spectacle on my blonde lashes, resembling a fantasy and imaginative kaleidoscope.

"I will cook something very special and vegetarian today. I'll call you later so you can come for dinner, my love," my mother said.

Sam replied, surprised, "I can't wait to try your dinner, dear."

That evening, Eugenia finished cooking and decorated the table beautifully. She sat me in the highchair and served wine and fresh pineapple juice. Sam arrived, drying his hands, and sat down, sweeping his hair to one side with a genuine and friendly smile. My mother, arranging the dishes on the table, said, "I was given this recipe that looks like meat, but it's a very fibrous vegetable seasoned with lots of spices. I hope you like it." And she served him a delicious plate of peppers and mushrooms, onions, and strips of well-seasoned vegetable "meat", all accompanied by steaming rice, which created a gentle mist beneath the lamp. They looked at each other, raising their glasses of red wine for a toast. Eugenia had forgotten one detail, the music, so she quickly got up and put on a Bill Evans vinyl. Then they danced and drank until I fell asleep on the couch, playing with my inflatable deer, one of those first inflatables made in China during its desperate mission to revive its economy and conquer the world.

In the morning, my father got ready to go to work. He gently opened the door to give me a glance and a blown kiss, then bid farewell to my deeply sleeping mother with a smile. Like every other day, Sam took a moment before closing the gate to greet the herd of animals and make sure they had enough water in case the day was too hot. Before opening the door of his brown VW Beetle, he closed the gate and noticed that something was missing. He turned around, went back, and searched everywhere for Baba.

As he turned the corner of the front yard, he noticed a puddle of blood gathering drop by drop beneath the post that held the small trash bin. Cautiously, he approached, untied the knot, and looked inside the bag. With its turquoise eyes half-closed and its tongue sticking out, the decapitated head of my beloved snow-white lamb peered out. My father retied the knot of the bag and tried to tie his own throat to stifle the sobs. He hurriedly walked to the gate with a face flushed with helplessness, his eyes holding back tears. When he raised his bewildered head, he came face to face with the nanny, who had just arrived to take care of me and attend to the household chores.

"Mamina, please take the garbage bags and immediately dispose of them at the municipal dump in the corner plaza. Clean the area with water to avoid attracting flies. Thank you, have a good day," he said.

He lowered his head again and angrily got into his car. On his way to the office, Sam couldn't help but replay in his mind the image of

Baba's bloodied head, while sweet images of his daughter and the child playing together like siblings, even sharing bottles of "Nido" milk, kept crossing his mind. Suddenly, he remembered the "vegetable meat." He stopped the car next to some bushes by a dirt soccer field, quickly got out, and vomited until his soul felt empty.

Tormented and fed up with his wife's strange surprises, my father couldn't bear another day. He firmly believed that if he stayed, he would end up in a psychiatric hospital before she did. After taking a few weeks to make the decision, he spoke to Mamina and entrusted her with taking care of me. He promised to send her money for whatever she needed, took her hand, and placed a piece of paper with an address and phone number in it, asking her to keep that information as sacred as a relic. Mamina tucked the paper inside a book on the living room shelf.

The next morning, as normal, my father quietly entered my room, ran his fingers through my hair, and kissed my forehead. That night, he didn't come home but returned to Paris. I never saw my father again, and over the years, I always remembered that I had been very happy by his side and that, in his own way, he loved me.

Rapunzel

During that time, my smile faded away. My father, Baba, and even Mamina were no longer there. Mamina resigned due to the mistreatment from my mother. I felt very lonely, and my moments of happiness were only when I was close to my animal friends or when I could dream of beautiful things for myself, playing with handmade dolls crafted by local artisans. In these dreams, one doll represented me, and the other was my father, who would come flying like Superman and rescue me from this house and this loneliness.

On the other hand, Eugenia didn't feel lonely at all. Despite her outbursts and periodic suicide attempts, she made time to invite many people to the house. For a while, I had noticed that something was brewing amidst this constant coming and going. A military truck with wooden railings and a canvas roof arrived one day. At least ten uniformed men stepped out, their foreheads sweating, and their rifles slung on their backs. They started taking everything away.

"Here, take these bags and pack all your scraps. We're leaving. I won't take all your animals, so choose which ones go and which ones stay," my mother ordered me, while the soldiers, with the seriousness of a top-secret mission, continued loading furniture, lamps, and mattresses onto the olive-green truck. I was bewildered and confused. My heart raced as I put a collar on Ruby, my dog, and placed Leopold, a small monkey with brown eyes, a dark face, and orange fur, in a small cage. Leopold had been my laughter-filled friend for as long as I could remember, watching him climb on the goat and treat it like a horse was always a joy of mine.

My father had named him Leopold out of sympathy for the first democratic president of Senegal, Leopold Senghor, who had become an intimate friend of my mother.

Another truck parked outside the house to take boxes and baskets filled with Eugenia's collections along with pots and patio plants, followed by a black Peugeot sedan, from which another military officer stepped out, adorned with numerous medals, insignias, and symbols on his uniform, indicating a high-ranking official. He took off his cap and kissed Eugenia on each cheek, then stood by her side, embracing her shoulder with a perfect white smile, puffing his chest like a fighting rooster.

"What do you think, Eugenia? Efficient, isn't it? Are you pleased?" he asked.

"Yes, yes, thank you very much, Captain Satou. What would I have done without a man like you? Being such a lonely woman as I am! Please, tell your men that we will have refreshments upon arrival, and don't forget about the party I'm hosting on Saturday. I forbid you to miss it!" Eugenia replied.

The officer responded, "It will be an honor, dear Eugenia. I'll be there."

He saluted militarily, turned on his heel, and walked away with a steady and martial gait. Eugenia grabbed her purse, took my hand, and we got into the car, not my father's car, which he had given to a good friend, but hers—a orange-colored Volkswagen. I suppose they liked Volkswagens ever since they bought the green van that they had left stored in France; it was a brand of vehicle that, in a way, allowed them to have something in common, their wanderlust and love of the hippie style.

After about twenty minutes, we parked in front of that castle that made her father, the former general, sigh during his last unexpected visit. Eugenia ran back and forth, directing the Senegalese troop of soldiers, instructing them where each piece of furniture should go.

"This is your room, Andrea. Bring your things down and start organizing," she said.

I brought Ruby and Leopold into my room, and we waited. Leopold climbed onto the window, which had iron bars and overlooked the backyard. The backyard was spacious and filled with fruit trees. I could also see a decorative pool with a naked African child pouring water from a jug, but it was empty, with white paint cracking like dry scales in the sun. The floor of that patio was not tiled like in our humble previous house; instead, it consisted of natural stone pieces with cement grouting between each one. It looked rustic and artisanal, and María Eugenia was fascinated with her new outside floor. I suppose due to the humidity, many walls were affected at their base with mold. And those medieval-looking walls were also begging for a fresh coat of paint. My room was light blue, with an antique mirror hanging on the wall, a dusty General Electric desk fan anchored in a corner of the ceiling, my bed, and a bedside table. I kept my clothes in suitcases and boxes under the tall-legged bed with brass knobs.

Eugenia had bought the property and had been secretly working on completing the rest of the house. She hired some local masons who built a tower attached to the walls, featuring the same medieval defensive architecture and small windows at the top that seemed like the perfect movie set for Rapunzel.

The soldiers had completed their mission and were sitting in a row under the shade of the wall facing the street. A couple of women had arrived and were serving bissap, a refreshing hibiscus infusion with a highly perfumed and pleasant flavor. The women smiled as they served the drink because it was well known that the flower was a good aphrodisiac and energy booster for intimate moments among Senegalese people. Apparently, it was also ideal for free moves with the help of influential figures and fiscal resources sponsored by Leopold, not the monkey, but the President of Senegal himself.

We started painting the house in a pale pink color, and painting became one of my first obligations. Inside that castle, things happened that I will never forget and that left a lasting mark on my life.

I began attending school in the city, and my mom rarely dropped me off or picked me up from there. I usually took a bus or walked for about forty minutes. The buses of that time didn't have air conditioning. And apparently, they didn't have shock absorbers either because it felt like being inside a mobile oven, where the constant movement could dislocate bones, jostle eggs out of baskets, glasses, and dentures, or if someone fell asleep by the window, they would wake up with a bump on their forehead, among other common accidents. That was one of my favorite moments of the day when I looked out the window and could travel with my imagination to other places, explore the Chile I had always heard about, Paris, or Disneyland in the United States. Sitting on that bus, I could observe people from a different perspective, I could observe the traders, the cyclists who, as they passed me, made me turn my head to watch them disappear at the end of the avenue. I could see the sea and its fishermen slowly emerging and disappearing amidst the tide's ebb and flow. It allowed me to see this town from a different dimension, a town that was able to gain its independence but was left with a legacy of language mixtures, religions, beliefs, and traditions. From the French and English languages to dialects of more remote tribes, to modern churches and even the most indigenous and ancient Mandinka santerías, it possessed an irreplicable, confusing yet unique identity.

Chaman

As I reached the age of five, my father's memories still remained, but gradually I had grown accustomed to his absence. My mother would always tell me he was a wretched bastard who had abandoned us, and that a curse hung over the memory of that man, with which she constantly had to contend. She would light candles, bring out pumpkin bowls, and pour chicken blood into them. She would write her scribbles and insults in French on scraps of paper, tearing them up and emptying them alongside spits of rum and herbs she brought from the continent's interior. She would put on a white dress and robe, adorn herself with a necklace made of animal claws, assume a Hindu-style Padmasana position, and then extend her arms with palms facing upwards. She would start speaking in dialects I couldn't comprehend, and her eyes would rapidly blink, turning white. She would then dip her fingers into the potion inside the pumpkin and draw serpentine lines on her arms. She would smoke and blow the smoke in all cardinal directions, and then came the trance and the dance.

The only thing she didn't add to the potion, as they were the appetizers prior to the ceremony, was the string of smuggled pills that transformed her and turned her into a professional macumbera. I was very frightened by her state and preferred to watch her from hiding in the kitchen or the corner that faced my room. Often, other women would join her in these ceremonies, and together they would perform a ritual worthy of recording, as the house became filled with smoke, seeds, blood, and a mess of objects, candles, and incense. Men would also come, and after the ritual, they would stay until late, and I wouldn't see them leave. For some strange reason my mother had a habit of placing me next to these men and women and taking photos of us. Sometimes she would dress me up in costumes and force me to pose with these people, though I wasn't sure of her intentions. It frightened me. She was also fascinated with positioning herself seductively among the men on the couch, encouraging them to photograph her.

With the passing of time and her growing madness, she began to convince her cursed dragon that I was the cause of all her woes. I was the wretched burden and responsibility imposed on her by that man who had abandoned her. I was practically the living curse that brought all the misfortunes of the world into her life. Perhaps it was because she named me "Fabi" after Andrea, defying the orders of Ifa, the chieftain. I was her and she was Sergio, reflected in a mirror fractured by time and her withered dignity.

I can't recall the reason or motive, but I do remember when she first struck me. Without any consideration for my size, fragility, and innocence, she thrust her fist, adorned with afro rings, into my left eye, inflicting a large and deep cut on the upper part of my cheek as I was about to leave the kitchen to play in the yard. I fell backward and nearly lost consciousness. Panic and terror seized me to such an extent that I couldn't scream or cry. I lay there on the floor, gazing at the central lamp that resembled an aerodrome for flies, barely breathing, obtuse, and understanding nothing, as if wandering in an infinite space where only fear, horror, and utter confusion dwelled. I turned my head to see her thick-heeled flamenco dancer shoes disappear through the front door, followed by a violent slam that compressed the air, momentarily freeing the lamp from the swarm of flies. She left, perhaps shouting obscenities at me, and slowly, I struggled to get up, dragging myself to seek refuge in my room, while my cheek throbbed with heat, inviting pain to consume me entirely. Despite always playing with my animals and the soil, I lacked the presence of mind and wisdom to clean the wound. I only managed to grab a dirty piece of clothing from the bed to staunch the bleeding. That night and the following ones, I couldn't sleep due to the pain. The wound became infected, and a pus-filled lump grew, causing severe swelling that impaired my vision. I was on the verge of losing sight in my left eye, and there was no one to come to my aid. My desperation took hold of my consciousness, preventing me from even thinking. All that remained was my instinct for survival, the only thing to which I clung.

After a week of silence, Eugenia grabbed me by the chin, glanced at her art masterpiece, grabbed her purse, and took me to a shoddy healer "shaman". It was a rundown shack that couldn't quite pass for a cabin or a house, and the man sat inside, next to a smoldering brazier upon which he dropped damp herbs, producing thick smoke. Above his head hung dead and stiff birds, rats, snakes, and monkeys, bundled with seeds and tree bark. It was a funereal place, dark, carpeted with cowhides, and it smelled of dried meat, greasy soil, and cemetery. The man, with dry and wrinkled skin, whom I could only partially see through the ceaseless smoke of the cigarette in his mouth, chanted a few stanzas of some long-lost song, shook some shrub branches around me, and then, without anesthesia or the necessary sanitary measures, made an incision and began to extract the pus, reducing the inflammation in my cheek. Afterwards, he applied a brown liquid and placed a patch with herbs to cover the entire area. In the following weeks, the wound improved, but the scar remains to this day. The shaman, while unquestionably an unsanitary character with an undesirable clinic, at least had the wisdom to save my eye.

Since that time, Eugenia's wayward dragons found some delight in the suffering of others, a release for their repressed emotions, an escape that allowed their imagination to come to life, providing her with a sense of relief that sometimes manifested as a smirk or a deep sigh of satisfaction. Gradually, she discovered that it wasn't so difficult to make everything appear as an accident; all she needed was to reach into her wallet, her lies, her bipolar nature, or her influences. Somehow, she believed that I would never report her, resurrecting the words her own father had once said to her: "Who would believe a whore like you?"

Every few days, I would get into the car with her, and we would go to the supermarket in the city center. I would wear loose dresses and a backpack, and we would start walking through the aisles, with her indicating the items I had to hide in my clothes and bag. Then, she would go to other aisles, leaving me alone to carry out the misdeed. She, on her part, a true artist of the spontaneous disappearance of things, took care of the whiskey bottles, perfumes, and makeup. But there came a time when someone saw me and reported me, and without realizing it, within ten minutes, I had a couple of police officers behind me, caught red-handed. Regardless of my age, they arrested me and took me to the police station, locking me up in a fetid, damp, and dark cell. Meanwhile, my mother was nowhere to be found. The officers asked me all the relevant questions to ascertain my identity and then located my mother, who had already returned home to stash her own loot after seeing from a distance how I was being apprehended. When she arrived at the police station, they brought me in front of her, and as soon as she saw me, she started shouting:

"How could you, Andrea?! How dare you jeopardize my reputation like this. It's shameful!" She gathered momentum and slapped me in front of everyone.

"Never do it again, do you hear me? Or I'll burn your hands for being a thief."

They released me, and after having her sign a few documents, we went home without saying a word to each other. The shame, humiliation, and anger were so overwhelming that I seriously considered poisoning her with rat poison as revenge. But just the thought of the poison not working and the risk of being discovered terrified me, so I abandoned my plans.

Years later, I learned that she also forced my father to put things in his pockets, telling him it was "exciting" to do so.

Sacred Readings

My mother was so immersed in the studies of African cultures and traditions that she forgot about my Christian baptism and assigned me an Islamic teacher. He was a large man with hands that showed little signs of labor. He dressed in the purest Muslim fashion, wearing sandals that made his well-kept and clean feet visible. He also had a distinct scent, a mix of wood, sweat, and tobacco, and I know this because I sat beside him for two hours each day studying the Quran. He was an educated and kind man towards both of us. Before leaving, he would spend some time conversing with my mother at the garden gate. I never saw or knew how much she paid him for his services.

Sometimes, I would feel very sleepy while reciting the teachings of Muhammad, and when I began to nod off, instead of waking me up or scolding me, the teacher would fall silent and watch me as I drifted to sleep. Then I would jolt awake and resume reading. Eugenia was loving and exemplary as a mother during our classes, even serving us refreshments and English butter cookies. I believe that attention during the classes were the only displays of affection I received from her during my childhood. I cannot recall a hug, a kiss, a joke, or any sense of camaraderie between mother and daughter during our time together. Perhaps that is why I developed an affection for the prophets and their teachings. The teacher even had me read some references about Jesus in the Quran, and I found myself confused, wondering if he was the same figure from the Bible or if it was merely a similarity in names. I never asked the teacher, as I didn't want to make him feel uncomfortable, in case there were two gods with different sons but the same name.

During a certain week, my mother got lost in the jungle again and did not return for three days. By then I was almost 7 years old, capable of making myself a sandwich and proficient in feeding Ruby and Leopold, so no one went hungry. Besides, it had been a long time since we had a nanny, so through Eugenia's shouts and military-like orders, I learned how to manage, cleaning and tidying the house, sweeping the patio, washing dishes and laundry, making the bed, watering the plants, carrying bricks, painting, weeding, and everything else.

Professor Abdou came to my reading that summer afternoon. I had come back from school and changed my clothes. I put on a beige cotton robe and tied my hair up. When he entered, I greeted him as usual and offered him a coffee, which he gladly accepted to beat the heat. I turned on the fan in the living room, and while the water was heating up, we prepared the books on the table.

"What about your mother, Andrea?" he asked.

"Well, she went to work and didn't come back yesterday. She often does that and leaves me alone, but I'm sure she'll be back tonight or tomorrow."

"Poor girl, aren't you afraid of being alone at night?"

"No, Mr. Abdou, my animals take care of me."

He had already finished his coffee when he asked if he could use the restroom. I heard his footsteps as he left the bathroom, and I noticed that he veered towards the hallway leading to the guest room. He gently opened the door and then returned to the living room to continue our studies. I was reading when, without saying anything, he stood up, took me by the arms, and led me to that room. He threw me onto the bed and pounced on me. With one hand, he covered my mouth, almost suffocating me, and with the other hand, he lowered his pants and lifted my robe. I believed it was a dream, that what I was experiencing wasn't real. For a moment, I thought that he wasn't my teacher anymore but had transformed into a demonic giant whom I couldn't get off of me, no matter how hard I tried. I cried from intense pain, but also because no one in the world could rescue me, not Muhammad, not Jesus, not even Ruby, whom I couldn't call out to because my mouth was sealed shut by the giant's hand. He sexually assaulted me for at least five minutes until he abruptly withdrew from my tense and unresponsive body. When he finished his assault, he wiped himself with his own robe and slowly sat on the bed without looking at me. He sat at my feet and said:

"I hope this stays between us. It's our secret, and it's sacred because Allah has willed it so. If you tell anyone, you will sin and die. Understood?"

He stood up, went to the bathroom, took his books from the table, put them in his bag, and then left. I cried in the fetal position for a long time until I fell asleep. When I woke up, it was already night, and my mother hadn't returned yet. I managed to compose myself and went to take a shower, witnessing my childhood virginity turn into red streams of water flowing down my legs and disappearing into the drain. I continued crying from fear and pain until the early hours of the morning.

The next day, bearing my new tragedy, I went to school and didn't speak a word to anyone. When I returned home, I saw my mother unloading suitcases and wooden boxes from a van. As soon as she saw me, she ordered me to help carry the boxes. I felt even more alone, deprived, and for the first time, I realized the vulnerability of women and girls in a society that was light-years away from discussing feminist rights or penalizing sexual assault.

I locked myself in my room and couldn't help but cry. My mother opened the door and upon seeing me, she said:

"Why are you crying now? Do you miss that bastard of a father of yours?"

I don't know where I found the strength, but I told her what had happened. Eugenia bit her lips, rolled her eyes, pulled her hair, and clenched her fists.

"I'll be right back, don't move from here, Fabi!"

I heard the familiar sound of the air-cooled motor of the Beetle starting and then accelerating violently until it disappeared, mingling with the dust of the street along with my mucus and tears. When she returned many hours later, she didn't come with the police or the rapist. She simply arrived and ignored me. From that moment on, she didn't speak to me for a week, and the only times she addressed me were to order me to buy her pills or medicine, or to clean this or that, or to organize the kitchen.

One afternoon, she sent me to the pharmacy to buy Diazepam. At the store next door, I read on the front page of the local newspaper that the day before, Professor Abdou had been raped and murdered inside the prison where he had been incarcerated, and the causes and perpetrators of the attack were unknown and under investigation.

"Have you seen the newspaper, Mom?"

"Yes, Andrea, I already knew."

"You made them kill him, didn't you?"

"It's your fault, Andrea. You killed him."

She locked herself in her room, screaming insults and throwing things. Then, as usual, she emerged from her hiding place and rushed to grab a glass of whiskey. She lit a cigarette and sat on the sofa, where she remained until nightfall. Suddenly, I heard her strumming her guitar, but it only produced a couple of notes before she violently threw it to the ground. That sent shivers down my spine, and I knew that one of the dragons had awakened.

I was locked in my room, writing an aimless letter to someone who didn't exist when I heard my mother shout, "Fabi, come here!".

My heart started pounding, and I cautiously approached the living room where she had just finished a cigarette and was lighting another with trembling hands, her back turned as she stared out the window.

"Take off your clothes, I'm going to examine you," she ordered me.

Once I undressed, she grabbed my arm, swept the tablecloth off the table with a sudden movement, and forced me to lie down on it. Hanging from the chair, she had previously prepared several colorful pieces of craft rope. She tied my arms and legs to the table legs. My desperate breaths nearly suffocated me. I felt my chest being crushed and tried to lift my head to see what Eugenia was doing in the kitchen while futilely attempting to free myself from the restraints. I thought she might be searching for a flashlight or magnifying glass to examine me, but then I heard the sound of the metallic cutlery drawer. Next, I heard the stove being ignited, and from there, in her intoxicated and demonic state, she began shouting at me.

"You are the cause of this misfortune, you provoked it!" she exclaimed, and hurried back with a butter knife, its tip glowing red in her hand. "This will make you lose any desire to tempt like a whore!"

With all her strength, she forcibly spread my thighs and pressed the burning red knife against the outer lips of my vagina. I screamed so loudly that I couldn't hear what she was shouting or the curses and insults that escaped her mouth because my voice was stronger, shrill, and dissonant compared to hers. The pain was unbearable, and I fainted, transitioning from hearing her distant curses to a deadly silence.

When I awoke, it took me a moment to adjust to consciousness and accept that everything that had transpired was not merely a nightmarish figment. Concurrently, as I reacquainted myself with reality, the pain began to seize hold of me.

Eugenia had released me from my restraints and carelessly discarded my garments upon my abdomen. The agony was so acute that I yearned to let out another scream, yet I suppressed the impulse, wary of attracting her attention. Fortunately, I discerned that she was no longer within the confines of our abode. With considerable effort, I rose to my feet and, moving with deliberate slowness akin to a penguin, made my way to the bathroom to cleanse and soothe the scalded flesh. It represented the most harrowing torment I had ever conceived of enduring, and within my juvenile psyche, I remained incapable of fathoming the rationale behind my mother's aberrant transgression.

What had I done? Where lay my culpability? In what manner had I erred this time? Such thoughts plagued my mind, their resolutions eluding me. For heaven's sake, I had been the victim of a violation, not the perpetrator, regardless of the deity invoked—be it God, Allah, Mohammed, or any other!

My panic towards that woman consumed me entirely. I started locking myself in my room, fearing that she would enter at the most unexpected moment to kill me. My nights were overwhelmed by incessant thoughts and nightmares, and the pain was relentless. I was terrified at the thought of the wound getting infected, as had happened before with my eye, so I took great care to keep the injury clean and disinfected. If that were to happen, I wouldn't know how to resist my mother before she took me back to that quack doctor. Healing silently and completely became my priority for many weeks.

The Red Light

One of those nights, I heard people arriving, men and women. My mother sang with her guitar, and toasts could be heard constantly, followed by laughter and music. All I could do was put the pillow over my head in an attempt to find some sleep. In the early hours of the morning, the party started to die down, and I could barely hear murmurs coming from the living room, and sometimes people walking towards the other rooms or the bathroom. When I momentarily removed the pillow from my head, I noticed a faint red light seeping in from under the door. I got up, almost holding my breath, and pressed my ears against the door to listen to those strange moans and groans. I thought that if everyone was drunk and asleep, this would be my best chance to go to the bathroom and avoid Eugenia's reprisals the next day for interrupting her party by not being able to hold my needs. I cautiously and very slowly opened the door and peered out with my heart in my hand, ready to cross the hallway. Amidst the stale air filled with cigarettes and alcohol, with subtle shades of red, black, and purple gliding over a mass of bodies, I could see my mother with other naked men and women intertwining and moving slowly with each other like shiny, moist octopuses. I turned my head towards the living room, where other people were having sex between the sofa and the floor. I stealthily crossed to the bathroom and then returned without turning my head in any direction. The panic of just the thought that one of those people might enter my room and try to do what Professor Abdou did to me, invaded every cell of my being, so after lying down, I got up again to barricade the door with my chair and anything within reach without making any noise. Only then could sleep overcome my paranoia and desperation. *Where are you, Dad?* It was the only question that came to my mind.

My mother rented a P.O. box at the central post office, and once or twice a month, she would go there to pick up mail. Occasionally, I would discreetly spy on her from some corner of the house when she sat on the couch to open the letters and packages. Sometimes she would take out candies, chocolates, and photographs. She would read the letters and tear them up, while others she wouldn't even bother to open. Perhaps one of those letters came from my father, who at that time had become a Touareg once again, wandering on adventures, this time in Germany.

Samuel ran into an old French friend who invited him to participate in a lucrative but risky business of smuggling marijuana and hashish between Europe and America. Together with the rest of the gang, they performed the most creative tricks to elude customs and the police. In Germany, Sam had met a woman who was helping him forget his troubled past alongside Eugenia. He had fallen in love once again. Her name was Monika. She had a daughter named Melanie with a black man with whom she never formed a family.

One day, his friend gave him all the instructions to finalize an important marijuana shipment, and they agreed to meet the buyers and make the arrangements at a less crowded train station on the outskirts of Hamburg. Sam was very nervous and told his girlfriend about the plans, promising her that they would reunite soon in New York. She, with a much stricter disposition than his, immediately put him between a rock and a hard place.

"Choose. It's either your friend or me. If you go to that place, forget about me," she warned him.

After listening to his intelligence more than his spirit of adventure, Sam scratched his head and wisely chose her. That afternoon, his friend and the rest of the gang were captured by the German police. In no time, Sam, Monika, and her daughter flew to New York, and there, his new life began, back in his home country. After some time, they started a family by conceiving another daughter, whom they named Katie.

As Sam's adventurous spirit began to calm down, my grandparents returned to Dakar for a visit, for the second time. I still walked with difficulty, careful not to accidentally disturb the scabs from the burn inflicted by my mother.

"Walk properly, understood? Don't you dare walk strangely in front of my parents," she commanded. "Nor should you ever tell them what has happened to you, or you will lose out, do you hear me?"

During that visit, I grew closer to my grandmother Teresa, who was the only person besides my father who had shown any affection towards my existence. Teresa would invite me to her guest room, the same room where the monster Abdou disobeyed the sacred scriptures, and she would sit by my side, combing my hair and braiding it.

"What happened to your eye, my love? Why do you have that scar?" she asked.

After a brief palpitation and careful consideration of my response, I said, "I fell while playing with Ruby, Grandma."

With them, I could escape for a few hours and experience life as other children did, playing on the beach, eating fruit ice cream, and even having them buy me girls' clothes and other gifts. During my grandparents' stay, my mother became a perfect woman, cheerful, but above all, the queen of hypocrites. One Friday, we went to dine at a luxurious restaurant in the city center, where I remember sitting at an elegant table, and important figures would occasionally pass by, stopping to greet my mother and my grandparents. At that point, I made every effort to walk without the slightest hint of my intimate problem being noticed, and on top of that, I had to smile and appear happy in front of the Senegalese families and social elite.

When we arrived home, my grandmother, perhaps due to a few too many drinks, was suffering from a headache that forced her to retire to her room. Eugenia didn't hesitate to grab a couple of African pills and a glass of water, offering them to her mother, who fell asleep like a bear in Russian winter.

"It's time to sleep, Andrea, say goodbye to your grandfather," Eugenia said to me with strange kindness.

"Goodnight, my dear, rest well. Tomorrow we'll go out for a walk," my grandfather Sergio said.

"Goodnight," I replied and closed the door to my room.

I fell asleep, thinking about the next day, imagining that I would return to being a happy child with a normal life despite everything, without realizing how far I was from improving my emotional and psychological situation. Around three hours later, I woke up feeling very thirsty from the "thiéboudiene" I had eaten and decided to go to the kitchen for a glass of water. As soon as I sat down in my bed, I could see that soft red light once again slipping under my door. Confused and trying to shake off my sleep, I placed my ear against the door and heard moans of a man and a woman, very similar to the ones from previous times when María Eugenia invited her fan club. Cautiously, I stepped out into the hallway, which smelled of tobacco and African patchouli perfume. Faint music was coming from my mother's room. I took a deep breath and tiptoed towards that room, my fingers grazing the wall to maintain balance. My concentration on making no noise was so intense that I completely forgot about the discomfort of my wounds. With my finger, I pushed the slightly ajar door open further until I could see the mahogany vanity with its large framed and beveled mirror and delicately carved drawers. That mirror and my eyes bore witness to something my mind could not believe or understand. General Castillo was mounted on my mother like a wild dog, holding her hair with one hand and gripping her wide hips with the other. He whispered things into her ear that I couldn't hear, and when he finished speaking, she emitted muffled guttural screams that I couldn't determine whether they were cries of pain or part of the ritual. Then he fell back, panting intensely, and she straddled him, moving like a snake in a trance. Holding my breath and my astonishment, I slowly retreated until I reached my room, where I lay down again and remembered how thirsty I was. But after witnessing that scene, I preferred to endure until the next morning.

I felt disgust, repulsion, hatred, sadness, and a deep sense of powerlessness as the images I had just witnessed replayed in my mind over and over again. I thought I had to do something to help my mother escape from the clutches of that man, but at the same time, I thought that if she was going through the same terrible circumstances I had experienced with Mr. Abdou, at least she deserved it for everything she had done to me. So, I abandoned the desire to help her as the pain from my wounds returned, and in trying to endure it, I fell asleep.

Two weeks passed during which I heard the same noises on several nights, and the red light seeped under my door. I wanted to tell my grandmother, but it was too risky. I thought that if I did, Eugenia and her father would end up killing us and making us disappear. But there were situations and behaviors from my grandmother that I didn't know how to explain, and I could only conclude that she was very much aware of what was happening, but she kept quiet about it, serving the silence as a feast to indifference. The remaining fragments were kept in a corner she had in her heart for the pain and anguish that had been with her for a long time.

Many years later, I grew tired of searching for answers or fully understanding those powerful psychic forces capable of dominating a person's mind to the extent of forming emotional bonds with their abuser, as was the case with Eugenia and her father. The only thing I could conclude was that somehow my mother managed to absorb and make her victimhood disappear by channeling it through a complex mental mechanism that allowed her to transform her trauma into a self-accepted romantic relationship in order to continue living a semi-normal life. Perhaps she tried to erase her disturbed past by forcing herself to be a strong and balanced person alongside Samuel, and in the process, her cursed dragon grew fat and hungry for revenge. And in the end, without any intention of thanking my misfortune, I was the only one paying the price for it all. It has been very difficult for me to erase those moments, and it's not surprising.

The matter concluded with a cold farewell this time. My grandmother Teresa hugged me tightly and gently ran her finger over the scar on my eye, as if convincing herself that I had lied about my accident with Ruby, and she gave me a smile followed by a kiss. My grandfather hugged me and looked at me with a mix of seriousness and shame. My mother took them to the airport, and I was once again left alone in this silent and cruel castle.

As they left, my mother forgot to lock her spacious bedroom. I was strictly forbidden to enter without her consent, and the few times I did, it was just for a quick in and out to bring her something or receive orders. Nonetheless, my fear of my mother had grown to the point where I had no intention of entering, and I tried my best to only go as far as the door. But that day was like an irresistible invitation to take a casual glance, which I couldn't resist, and I dared to enter, dodging the disorder, ignoring the prohibition, and risking my life.

The room was filled with the most incredible objects from the indigenous peoples she knew. Many ceremonial masks, bows and arrows, textiles, and photographs were hanging on the walls. Stone sculptures adorned the fine furniture, and on the bedside table, I could find everything from incense to a gorilla skull, dandelion teeth, various utensils like mirrors, knives, and ivory elephant combs. I explored her room, and the room explored me. On her nightstand, there was a collection of medicines, and in the partially open drawer, I could see two guns and cardboard boxes filled with bullets. In one corner, there was another piece of furniture filled with glasses with remnants of alcohol, perfume bottles, and ashtrays filled with lipstick-stained cigarette butts. Hanging from one of the ornamental bed legs was a leather whip and many silk handkerchiefs, while on the floor beside it, the remains of what was once a beautiful cheetah, and on the opposite side, also lying on the floor like a carpet, the remnants of a zebra. Under her bed, there were many boxes and bags filled with photographs, clothes, documents, and tribal objects. She also had scattered jewelry and precious stones everywhere, earrings, rings, bracelets, and necklaces, and of course, a large number of black pencils, both new and used, to outline her eyes. Despite the heat of that day, a chill ran down my spine as I visited that room. My mother had instilled so much fear in me that without realizing it, I no longer saw her as my mother but as a stranger who held me captive in her own madness, from which I couldn't escape.

Once I stopped walking like Chaplin, I started going to school again, while my mother, if she wasn't visiting some remote place on the continent, was attending social gatherings with authorities, politicians, academics, or businessmen of the country. At this point, she had completely abandoned Western clothing and merged into this unique and different society, displaying vibrant textiles that immediately showcased her class and lineage. She was the queen of Africa who never appeared in history books. Although I'm sure that if she had been born in Alexandria a century before Christ, she would have had her own pyramid.

And just as Cleopatra means "Glory of her father," she would have claimed the name for herself, and rightfully so.

Sometimes I have thought that Eugenia found in this cultural tapestry the perfect tools and society to vent her delusions and existential sorrows in a way she couldn't have found anywhere else in the world. Moreover, she built this castle to carry out her rituals and macumbas without interruption from anyone with a different logic. I vividly remember the times when, due to small details or errors in my household chores, I ended up bound and chained to a post that she had installed in the tower of this deranged castle. It resembled a medieval castle tower, with a small surveillance or ventilation window at the top, barred with metal grates, and access required climbing a considerable number of steps. Simply sweeping the entrance poorly and having her certify it by running her finger across the floor was enough for the deranged dragon to awaken and suggest chaining me in that place.

Many times, it wasn't enough for her to strip me naked and insult both me and my father at the same time, as if I were to blame for her failed relationship, and then abandon me for days on end. When anger possessed her or she became enraged by my screams for her to release me, she would go to her room and retrieve the whip hanging from the leg of her bed. She would lash my back and legs like Portuguese or English slave masters lashed their slaves. It was almost a pleasure for her to whip my body, and lines of ecstasy and relief would appear on her face, as if those moments were therapies that made her feel powerful and limitless. But she was no fool and never went too far as to break my skin. She wisely determined her limits, unlike a hitman or a serial killer who always has an urgency to eliminate and make their victim disappear as soon as possible. For instance, Ted Bundy and María Eugenia shared being very charismatic individuals, but unsuspectingly crazy, although they clearly differed in their techniques and modus operandi.

On many occasions, when she would go on her research trips, I would take advantage of the opportunity to escape to the beach and bathe in the salty sea to heal my hidden wounds and scars beneath my dresses.

María Eugenia was a bipolar woman who was extremely calculated in her words, gestures, and comments. To everyone she met in her social circle, she came across as a serious and trustworthy woman, a model citizen of integrity and example, just like my grandfather Sergio.

Only I, my father, and a few other victims came to knew how unpredictable she could be. At the same time, she was reserved and conservative towards those who didn't align with her ways, like me, and that's why I never had the opportunity to discover her weaknesses that could have been my allies. I also failed to fully understand her restless and traumatized world. Sometimes she would sink into her solitude, surrounded by her photographs, recordings, and notes from African expeditions, meticulously reviewing them amidst collections of coffee cups—some empty, some half-drunk, and some with lipstick stains and cigarette remnants floating in the concoction's dregs. I often saw her sinking amidst a thousand articles of African heritage from different regions, and seeing her, I imagined that she was inside a bubble, in silence, completely isolated from the world and sometimes even from life itself. Then she would fall into such a deep sleep that I didn't know if she was alive or dead.

She would take photographs of these objects, measure them, and write down their origin, material, original name, associated ethnicity, and meticulously note the purpose of each item, whether it be a piece of jewelry, a musical instrument, an amulet, or a ritual or decorative garment. She could spend hours and hours classifying her findings, and then that same night, she could organize a party that would end in a wild orgy, only to appear impeccably dressed at a gala the next day, hosted by some ambassador or another. She could transform herself into a prostitute at night and a distinguished professional during the day, effortlessly dodging headaches with a few pills. She had several lovers, and not just men.

I remember a Brazilian woman with voluptuous curves and disheveled hair, whom she called "Tatai Isabel," with whom she indulged in her hidden same-sex desires. Many lesbian women would come to these lascivious and lustful gatherings at our house, but the Brazilian woman had the most encounters with my mother. Often, especially on weekends, in the early hours of the morning, I would hear bossa nova music amidst moans and sexual cries emanating from their lesbian encounters. When my mother was preparing for a visit from Tatai Isabel, she would tidy up and clean her room, perfume it, and put on a Toquinho or Milton Nascimento record, that her friend had given her as a gift. The truth is that with her Brazilian company, my mother not only listened to the music of that country where she had lived and been so happy but also took the opportunity, amid body friction and interaction, to practice her Portuguese.

My mother was a very social person and often received visitors, and if she didn't, she would bring them using the most ingenious and unsuspected methods. One day she was talking on the phone, and without closing the door to my room, I paid attention to her conversation and even imagined the interlocutor's responses. With her stylized and elegantly resolute French, she said:

"So there are no charges against me anymore, right?" "You must understand that I am innocent, you know that. The weapon is registered, and I use it for personal defense." "That wretch is going to pay, even if he hides in the furthest corner of Mauritania." "I didn't drug him." "He was in love with me".

Immediately, I associated her conversation with that diplomat from Mauritania who used to come to see her on some suspicious nights. He was an elegant man, very well-dressed, with features so Arabic that he only needed a hump to resemble a camel, with his stylized beard, long legs, and penetrating dark eyes. I remembered that on some occasions, I saw him asleep in Eugenia's bed for many days until, on one of those days, while she was away, he woke up and started shouting desperately in his Semitic language, and the only thing he said in English was "Help, help!"

Scared by his desperation and not knowing what to do, I opened the door slightly and saw him tied up, completely naked, and sweating profusely. In order to avoid getting involved in matters that would bring me more trouble and to prevent myself from ending up locked in Rapunzel's tower in the same way, I had to be indifferent to what was happening and pretend that I never saw or heard anything. When my mother dressed him or covered him up a bit, she would send me to bring him food, telling me that he needed to be fed because he was sick. After several weeks with the man being held captive and drugged inside, one morning the police arrived and entered to "rescue" him, but not before arresting and handcuffing my mother and putting her in the police car.

"It's not what you think! Let go of me, you bastards, you have no idea who you're messing with, let go of me!"

Eugenia screamed as they pushed her, while others carried the half-naked camel on their shoulders. They briefly searched the entire house until they found one of the weapons, which they took in a bag. I watched everything from the patio and chose to continue playing the indifference game with my new friend who came to stay, a chameleon with beautiful colors and personality that I wanted to name Sam, but that name was forbidden. When the last officer closed the gate, I celebrated and thought, *"Finally, they caught this crazy woman, and she will pay for each of her sins."* But destiny, accompanied by the corrupt system, slapped my desires to the side, and that same night, the police car brought my mother back. In the following days, a local newspaper article read, "Mauritanian Diplomat Found After Weeks of Disappearance. The investigation has yet to reveal the names of the kidnappers or the motive behind the crime."

Senegal was a very corrupt place, and my mother knew exactly how to take advantage of that.

"Don't you dare tell anyone what happened, do you hear me, you brat? I only wanted to help that man, and he's alive because I took care of him. Now go clean the kitchen."

Letters And Pistols

My mother never celebrated my birthday. She never gave me a gift. She never told me a bedtime story, a joke, or gave any motherly advice. She was only my gendarme and often my executioner. She didn't take me out for a walk, let alone buy me an ice cream or a cake. Not even stolen ones. If I needed clothes, she would go and buy me pants and shirts to dress me as a boy. During the few times she took me out, apart from the delinquent visits to supermarkets, she would grab her purse, put a thermos with coffee, cookies, and her cigarettes, and order me to sit in the back seat of the Volkswagen. Then she would drive to some dark street, park, turn on the radio, lower the volume, and turn off the engine. She would then light a cigarette and stare fixedly at whoever entered or left a certain house. Sometimes a vehicle would arrive, a man would get out, and he would enter his house while my mother, very attentive, would stop chewing the cookie in her mouth or leave the coffee halfway and watch him from a distance without blinking, without missing any details. But sometimes hours would pass, and no one would enter or leave that place. Then she would become furious and drive like Fitipaldi to another street in front of a building to wait. If nothing happened after a few minutes, she would return to the previous street, and when she gave up spying without any conclusion, she would start driving aimlessly until I fell asleep and woke up when she slammed the door in front of our house at dawn. Her adventures with married lovers were a difficult puzzle to solve, but they made her feel more alive than collecting leather drums and wooden masks.

Every day I took Ruby for a short walk to do her business. Ruby knew that when I came home from school, she would have her moment to go out for a walk, and she eagerly awaited me. One day, Ruby had to wait longer than usual. My mother called me, and as always, I obeyed her commands militantly to avoid any punishment.

"Go to the pharmacy and tell Mr. Mamadou to send me a box of Valium. Take this money, don't lose it, and hurry up."

Mr. Mamadou wasn't there, and they didn't have that medicine. I was terrified at the thought of receiving a punishment if I didn't come back with her errand, so I ran to the next pharmacy several blocks away. Unfortunately, when I arrived home, she was standing with one hand on her waist holding her whip and a half-smoked Camel cigarette in the other.

"Why have you taken so long, you little girl?"

"I had to go to the other pharmacy..." I tried to explain, but she silenced me with a shout.

"Look what your damn dog has done, she has pooped on my stone floor and she will have to pay for it!"

Before she started whipping Ruby, I shouted:

"But Mom, I was late and couldn't take her outside, it's not her fault! Here's your medicine, please don't hurt her!" She snatched the pill box from me abruptly and continued.

"I don't care, someone has to pay for this! Choose, the dog or you!"

"Me! But please don't hurt her!"

She took one final puff of her cigarette, walked back to throw the butt in the ashtray by the entrance door, and then returned with a wicked smile. She grabbed me by the hair, forcing me to kneel, and forcefully shoved my face into Ruby's feces. Not content with that, she started kicking and whipping me wherever she could reach. My dog, agitated, whimpering and desperate with what was happening, didn't know how to defend me from my mother's aggression and could only jump around, confused and helpless, barking and yelping. She let go of me and walked away without saying a word. I was left lying there on her stone floor, trying to spit and get the filth out of my nose and mouth, holding back the urge to vomit. Ruby started cleaning my face with her loving and compassionate licks. This noble Belgian Groenendael friend was a gift from the Spanish ambassador in Dakar, who couldn't take her with him when he returned to his country. Initially, Eugenia didn't want her, but when she saw the instant connection, the dog made with me and we started playing, she had no choice but to accept the gift. My mother felt distance and rejection towards animals. A strange position for her, living in a land symbolized by its diversity of domestic animals and wildlife.

Not long after, she came up with the idea of tying Leopold to a tree with a chain so that he would stop jumping from tree to tree and scattering fruits everywhere. One day, my mother called a man to climb the tree and bring down Leopold, who was stiff as a mummy. He had suffocated while entangled in the chain. That day, I felt a lot of hatred towards my mother and at the same time, I thought that Ruby would be the next victim, and then it would be me.

I was terrified. Many options crossed my mind, escaping and running away on a boat, finding a way to gather money and pay someone to get me out of there, disguising myself to avoid being recognized. But all my plans and ideas were ruined when I thought that wherever I went, I would be recognized as the daughter of María Eugenia Castillo García Huidobro, the anthropologist and sociologist from Stanford, the researcher from IFAN, the daughter of the Chilean Army General, the daughter of the friend of the President of Senegal. To top it all off, my fair skin and golden blonde hair were not my allies in any sense, as they made me stand out too much during the day and night, making it impossible for me to escape without raising suspicion.

My sad and desperate heart couldn't find refuge anywhere in Senegal. My only friend from school was named Alexandra. She was the one I trusted enough to talk about the abuse from my mother and even show her my wounds. She told her mother about my situation, and since then, they both took care of me from a distance, with fear and without getting too involved. Of course, I didn't want to expose them to any danger, so I took all the precautions I could to meet them safely. Sometimes her mother intercepted us on our way back from school and brought a bag of food to feed me when Eugenia left me alone in the castle for weeks. Her mother understood the social position of mine very well and knew that reporting her to the local police would only result in retaliation and threats, and perhaps even the whole town and the priest turning against us. Alexandra's father was from Cape Verde, and at some point, they suggested taking me to the islands, but the risk of doing so could land them in jail since, even though Portuguese is spoken there and it is an independent state, it is closely linked to Africa and Senegal. Therefore, finding my trail would only be a matter of days.

At that time, after many years, my mother traveled to Chile and left me entrusted to her military friends and a military truck, with wooden seats, a wooden railing, and a canvas roof, which would come every morning to take me to school. I never saw anyone, but I could assure you that she also made someone available day and night to watch over me and take care of her castle in her absence.

Guillermina, the nanny of the Castillo García Huidobro family, had always been familiar with the secrets of the general's house, couldn't stand the parties or orgies. On that occasion, when Eugenia came to visit her father, Guillermina knew she had to close the door from the outside and keep her mouth shut once again. In a way, Guillermina was as conditioned as I was. And both of us were witnesses to the incestuous encounters. Without knowing each other, the taboo was the same for her in the Pacific as it was for me thousands of kilometers away in the Atlantic. My grandfather Sergio gave her a house. Now when I recount my story, I don't believe he did it to recognize Guillermina as a good domestic employee or for having raised his daughters Eugenia and Patricia, or for the years of service. Rather, I think it was in gratitude or as payment for her silence, and to provide her with a place to go during special occasions like Eugenia's visit or the nocturnal social parties.

Guillermina was a woman with great strength. I don't know if women still who endure everything in the name of honor or loyalty, but she saw things she shouldn't have seen and swallowed them one by one. And when I say that perhaps there are no women as "tolerant" as her, I say it because Teresa Paulina, my grandmother, went through the same and couldn't handle it.

Guillermina's endurance and resilience were such that she was able to gather the scattered pieces of my beloved grandmother's brains when she secretly took her husband's gun and shot herself in the mouth. My aunt Patricia, Sergio's favorite daughter, also didn't have the tolerance and fortitude of Guillermina and years later, she jumped from a building to end her life as well. At the end of the tragic equation, only the "tomboy" daughter and Pinochet's friend remained in the family. And I, as the sacrificial lamb, left to cleanse their sins.

Many years later, Guillermina would tell me about the things that happened during that time after Eugenia's arrival. These events very much mirrored my own experiences at home when during my grandparents' visits.

When my mother returned from Chile, she didn't even look at me. I made sure to receive her with the house clean and tidy for her arrival. All those household chores, from ironing clothes to watering plants, were moments for me to plan my escape, to remember Baba, Leopold, or the distant, blurry, and melancholic image of my father with his smiling beard, lifting me up to the sky with his strong arms. That same afternoon, my mother went to the post office and returned with many packages and letters. She kept all the correspondence in a locked trunk. She tore open some envelopes, threw things in the trash, then sat down, poured herself a glass of liquor, put on a Janis Joplin vinyl, lit a cigarette, and stared into the distance with vacant eyes until her glass was empty and her Camel turned to ashes. Then, very determined and with her head held high, she went to her room, came back with a piece of paper and a pencil, and forcefully placed them on the table, shouting:

"Andrea, come here!"

I was very nervous, knowing her tone and knowing that alcohol changed both her personality her soul. I watched her movements hidden outside from a window saturated with vegetation, and as soon as I heard her, I ran to her call.

"Yes, Mom?"

"Sit here, Andrea."

I sat in the chair with the paper and pencil in front of me, and from the corner of my eye, I saw her take out her revolver from her dress and place the barrel against my head. The mere touch of the metal against my skull made me feel smaller and more defenseless than the spirit of an ant resigned to be crushed into dust. My mind was barely able to command my hand to hold the pencil that trembled like wheat in the wind. Feeling the pressure of that revolver on my head, I closed my eyes, and in my imagination, I quickly said goodbye to all the beings I had loved in my short life. In those seconds, I only feared suffering and pain, not death, for death could be an immediate relief to my tragic life.

"I want you to start writing in your own handwriting:

Samuel Armstrong. You are a bastard dog who abandoned us. Forget about us and don't write or send me anything anymore. Forget about my mother and me, we are fine and happy. I am no longer your daughter, and I want nothing to do with you. Goodbye, Andrea Fabi."

I paid little attention to what I was writing because my biggest concern at that moment was not allowing a tear to fall on the paper and ruin it by diluting the ink. I'm sure that would have been enough for her to pull the trigger and then bury me in the backyard next to Leopold under the banana tree.

She snatched the letter, folded it in half, and put it inside an envelope. Then she went to her room, and after a few seconds, I was able to breathe again. I sat there, unable to move a finger, with my mind blank, dead inside. Suddenly, a fly landed on my hand, and at that very moment, I snapped out of my panic and trance, feeling a strange joy that I couldn't express. Through the words dictated by my mother, I suddenly realized that Samuel existed, that perhaps many of those letters and packages were for me. He hadn't forgotten or abandoned me! That letter written under the threatening gun was, in her drunkenness and without realizing it, a confession that managed to bring hope to my heart. My father was somewhere in the world and still thought of me! That letter was for him! Wake up, Andrea, wake up, you are writing to your father!

Paths Of Light

One summer day, my mother sent me to buy something. I don't remember the exact reason, but I was running late once again. I remember that upon my return, I opened the gate, took a few steps, and saw her coming towards me like an avalanche of fury. She had an iron pipe in her hand. Everything happened so quickly and chaotically that I couldn't evade her attack, and she hit me so hard in the head that the pain and the panic of feeling the blood run down my face prevented me from hearing what she was shouting at me or understanding why she was punishing me. My eyes trembled from side to side, uncontrollably, a dull and grave buzzing enveloped the terrifying image of my mother, blurry and gigantic, with her dark mouth that opened wide enough to swallow me. I felt everything moving up and down slowly, like an earthquake in slow motion. I felt like I was living the last moments of my life on a fishing boat, surrounded by dying fish bathed in blood, alone, in silence, being carried away by the ebb and flow of the tide.

Unaware of whether I was still alive or not, moving against the walls from side to side, I managed to reach my room. However, my last attempt to reach my bed was futile, and I collapsed onto the cold concrete floor, losing consciousness. A thin thread of warm blood slowly trickled down my temple, decorating the scene. I believe my mother was unsatisfied with the punishment, or perhaps she didn't derive enough pleasure from it because a few seconds later, she decided to follow me into the room to finish me off. I highly doubt she came to check on me, see how I was doing, or tend to my wound. I completely dismissed that possibility. All I could ascertain was that she saw me on the floor, bleeding out, and something chemical or magical happened in her conscience that awakened the gentle dragon within her, which either got scared or felt compassion for me. She tied a scarf around my head, covering my eyes, and took me to the hospital. I don't know how she did it; I wasn't there. I suppose she must have carried me to her orange truck herself and then ran to the emergency room. They shaved my skull, stitched me up with multiple stitches, and wrapped me up like a mummy.

I remember seeing translucent figures, illuminated by a purer than white light, like gentle flashes of an unknown sun that didn't hurt the eyes but caressed them like a balm of flowers. Everything felt normal and peaceful. Many people were smiling and others engaged in casual conversations, yet somehow connected in a collective state of well-being. I was searching for my father, and whoever I asked about him would smile or give me a caress through my blonde hair, which also shimmered like the sun, but they wouldn't respond to me. They guided me towards a path that widened like the horizon, stretching into an almost infinite spectrum. As I approached to take that route, I felt more accompanied and loved than ever before. I felt that everyone cared about me, that I was safe, and therefore, I didn't fear going further. On the contrary, I wanted to embark on the journey as soon as possible. I saw Baba, happy and blurred amidst the light, and far away, among white flowers, Leopold looked at me, pretending to be aloof but anxious and eager for me to run and embrace him. I started taking the first steps on that path of light when, at the same time, I began slowly opening my eyes and senses. At first, I heard a murmur of unrecognizable voices, and gradually, María Eugenia's voice became clearer as she spoke to someone. Immediately, out of instinct for survival, I preferred to keep my eyes closed to avoid her approaching me. Then, a profound sadness overwhelmed me at no longer being in that place from a few seconds ago. She was telling the doctor:

"We must do something, this cannot go unpunished. These boys on the street attacked my daughter just because she's white. That's racism, and I will do everything to seek justice! These criminals have no idea who they've messed with!"

Although I was still confused, after hearing her, my mind began to process everything. A tear started rolling down my cheek. It wasn't from pain or sadness. It was from powerlessness, anger, and not having the courage or strength to get up from that damn bed and scream in front of all the hospital staff that she had caused this, that she was a deranged criminal who had tried to kill me! Inside my silent self, I screamed until I was deafened, "She's lying, she's lying! She did it, that bitch!" I was very close to doing it, but I doubted that anyone would believe me, and if that happened, I couldn't imagine what would come next. Perhaps a horrific punishment or being locked up in a psychiatric hospital at my mother's request, just as my grandfather once threatened his daughter.

I gently clenched my jaws to contain the urge to expose her, and that slight movement reminded me, through sharp pain, that what she had done to me was more than a scratch. It was almost attempted murder. The next day, the doctor handed my mother a bag of medication, had her sign a few papers, and sent us home. She didn't utter a word throughout the entire journey. I got out of the car feeling dizzy and went straight to my bedroom, starting to feel tremendous pain and throbbing in my head. For several days, I would only get out of bed to fetch something to eat from the kitchen or the trees in the backyard, or to go to the bathroom. She never bothered to bring me food or check on my wound. The bloodstain on the floor of my room, despite washing it tirelessly, never vanished. It became a daily reminder that one day I wouldn't see the stain, this room, or anything else.

Sometimes, it wasn't enough for her to pull my hair, slap me, or hit me with whatever she found, including plates and shoes. She would lock me up in the tower for days without food, and if I opened my mouth, she would threaten to hang me and whip me until she got tired. The torture in Rapunzel's tower was special to her. She would wear a gratified smile every time she saw me suffer. I believe she felt like a Babylonian executioner, enforcing all the imbalanced and unjust laws of Hammurabi. That was my life, my routine. At times, I even thought that this was how things were supposed to be, and I started to believe that I was truly responsible for my mother's psychological trouble. I was born there, in that place. That was my home, my people, my nation. I shouldn't be ungrateful. On the contrary, no matter how painful it was, I should appreciate the life Eugenia gave me. Sometimes, I tried to euphemize my misfortune by thinking or whispering to myself, "It's your fault for abandoning us, Father." Perhaps the Stockholm syndrome, transmitted by my mother, also wanted to make me its captive patient.

Wild

They say that everyone is the master of their own destiny. But I wasn't even the owner of my own life, it depended on the chemical variations in my mother's brain! It also depended on the level of whiskey in her bottle of Johnnie Walker, the weather, how her day went, or who knows what other factors made her unpredictable and beyond my control. I don't know about destiny, but what I do know is that we are shaped by where we are born. Being born in a specific country can be a mere coincidence or a forced matter, like people crossing borders to escape wars, poverty, dictatorships, natural disasters, droughts, or political exile. In my case, it was the result of Sam and Eugenia's search to settle where it simply suited them better, where opportunities provided them with work and financial stability. It would have been just a matter of geographical distance if I hadn't been born a Frenchwoman, an American, or a Chilean. That's why I don't believe in the standards of nationalism, which often fall outside common sense and dress themselves in racism, classism, and hatred.

This untamed land simply saw me being born; from here, humanity was also born. This species had its first signs of existence when different groups of Homo sapiens roamed from the savannahs to the jungles, from the deserts to the oceanic coasts, with differences and similarities but clearly with identities and collective attributes closely linked to the environment they came from. There were short and timid ones, as well as tall and daring ones, thin and corpulent ones. Some were hairier, while others were smoother, all still unfinished, in the midst of the evolutionary process. We were small bands of nomadic families moving from one region to another in an annual circuit that followed the footsteps of animal species, both birds and mammals, and primarily the seasons of the year. Some groups had certain advantages over others; for example, some were accustomed to carrying spears and slings, while others shot from their bows at high speeds, others knew more advanced hunting and trapping techniques, while some were skilled fishermen or trackers.

We hunted and gathered what nature had to offer in a way that maintained an immutable and fair ecological balance. Many groups, clans, or tribes were lost to time, either becoming extinct or merging with more dominant groups. At the same time, the human species, through the amalgamation and fusion of DNA, was building that upright, capable of using its arms and hands for different functions than its legs and feet, ultimately creating the species that would dominate the face of the earth. Africa was populated first, followed by Europe, Asia, Oceania, and the rest of the continents. But the most common thread that these people of ancestral origins preserved and shared throughout the millions of years of evolution, which brought them together in communities, bands, or tribes, were their beliefs, myths, and stories. The sense of communion with nature in this region is also a key factor in understanding its different traditions and culture. Nature, to this day, is the primary ingredient shaping their perception of life and the world. Since ancient times, all goods and ills of individuals of the group were attributed to natural phenomena; animals, trees, and deities that existed only in the creative and imaginative mind of humans. Jaguars, thunder, rocks, plants, snakes and bats, elephants, mountains, the sun and moon, comets and meteorites, and countless other elements are the central pieces of the African cultural and religious puzzle. From there, stories, legends, and fables were born, passed down orally from generation to generation, repeated millions of times until they took on body, life, and spirit in the faith and belief of ancestral peoples, eventually becoming immutable truths over time. Voodoo, magic rituals, and santerías are deeply followed, respected, and celebrated by the vast African multitude. Contrary to the perception that may exist in other distant lands labeled as civilization, for them, these rituals are not about evil or perversion; quite the opposite, they represent hope, joy, improvement, healing, love, respect, and divine sacredness. While it is true that there are malevolent rituals, they are rare and isolated. Everything is a manifestation of spiritual needs or faith, just like confessing in a Catholic church, lighting candles on the Jewish menorah, going on a pilgrimage to the Virgin of Lo Vásquez, dancing a zapateado in front of the Virgin of Guadalupe, or placing messages without a destination in the Western Wall in Jerusalem.

My mother became involved in all these ancestral affairs, deeply rooted in African culture and began to live and experience it in her own way. She started finding meaning in what the Western world might call aberrations, sins, or savagery, ranging from tribes practicing polygamy, others marrying among women, some dyeing their hair yellow with cow urine, elongated lips and necks, ears deformed with clay plates and seed bracelets, body scarification or female genital mutilation, among many other customs that have managed to remain prevalent under an archaic halo.

The truth is that when I turned 13 years old and was on the eve of entering adolescence, Mrs. Castillo called me from her room. She was sitting on her bed with her Polaroid camera and told me that we should remember this date because I would soon become a woman.

"Take off your clothes and stay in your underwear," she ordered.

Almost robotically and without questioning her orders, I undressed beside the door, trying to cover my nudity with my hands.

"Look out and stand there. Stand up straight, girl, lower your hands, and now smile," she said as she took photos of me.

I waited for the automatic camera to spit out the first print. She shook it, blew on it, and threw it onto the bed.

"Now turn to face that wall, smile, girl, smile!"

The photos kept appearing, and her first reaction was to laugh, looking at me with a mocking smile. The next day, she went on a tour, perhaps to some corner of Africa, and didn't return for four nights. When she came back, she was accompanied by a man around 55 years old, dressed in a red tunic and brown garments around his waist. His dark skin shone under the sun, accentuated by the silver decorations. He carried a long staff, and a modern leather bag crossed his chest, contrasting with his native attire. He spoke a little tangled French and a different dialect than the Wolof I spoke, so I couldn't understand him. When he entered the house, my mother called me to the living room and ordered me to bring a glass of water to the gentleman. He smiled kindly, scanning me from head to toe with his slanted eyes, and once he finished drinking, he returned the glass with a smile that revealed teeth as white as the inside of tropical coconuts. His hands were not those of a laboring man, and his palms were the only distinct feature that stood out against the dark tone of his skin. He wore a necklace with a piece of raw solid gold, adorned with large black and red seeds. Then he opened his leather satchel, which he carried hanging from his shoulder, and took out some photographs, comparing them to me. He would look at a photo, then look at me and smile. He said a few things to María Eugenia, after which they concluded amicably by shaking hands. When I realized that they were the Polaroid photos my mother had taken of me, my white face turned pink with embarrassment and modesty.

The man took out a small, dark carved wooden stick with a snake leather handle from his bag, which was tied with seeds and herbs, and he gave it to my mother with a slight bow. He got up from the chair, approached me, caressed my cheek, turned around, and left, followed by my mother, who grabbed her bag and belongings and said to me, "I'll be back, water the plants." And she didn't return until the next day.

When I returned from school, she was sitting in the dining room, and as soon as she saw me enter, she said with an unusual smile, "You're a young lady now, Andrea, and you're going to marry the gentleman from the photos. He will take good care of you, and you will get along with his other wives. I hope you don't disappoint me."

She had sold me to this man from a small, isolated tribe in Senegal. I never knew if she exchanged me for money, land, or gold. The most common payment was in animals, but I'm sure Eugenia didn't accept that as payment since she disliked them to the point that she had killed almost all of mine. My days were numbered. I couldn't sleep from the horror of the thought that all this loneliness and bitterness I had lived for so many years would come to an end by marrying an old man from an ancestral tribe who didn't even speak my language. I couldn't accept or even imagine that soon I would become a tribal wife among other wives for the rest of my days. It was pure horror.

I thought about Professor Abdou and all that I had suffered, and the fear overwhelmed me at the mere thought that what was to come would be even worse. I was more alone than ever. The only solution would be to take my own life, and I had to do it as soon as possible. I started gathering the drugs my mother consumed, one by one, without her realizing what was missing. I needed a sufficient dose to end my life in one go because I was well aware that if, by some chance, I survived, I would receive a week of torture in the tower for jeopardizing my mother's deal with that man, and after that, I would be forced to marry him anyway.

But the days passed, and I saw no hurry or intention in my mother to get rid of me. I even thought that for some reason, the deal didn't work out, which gave me an advantage to carry out my suicidal plan. I never thought that the worst was yet to come, and it took me by surprise, ruining my entire strategy. Nor did I realize at that time that my mother would take cultural traditions so seriously, beyond what her work as an anthropologist assigned her.

After a few weeks, she arrived at noon with a woman from a village outside the city, evident from her attire, dialect, and clothing. My mother had her come into the living room, and together they moved the coffee table to the side, fully exposing the natural burlap cloth. The bald woman with her numerous bracelets and colorful clay and wooden earrings said something to my mother, and she hurried to the kitchen and brought a plastic tray with water and salt.

"Come closer, Fabi, lie down here. You're getting married, and this lady is going to prepare a remedy for everything to go well. Behave yourself..."

Surprised and overwhelmed with fear, I lay down on the cloth as the woman took out some herbs, and my mother set them on fire in a dish, letting them smoke. I was only wearing a tunic and my cotton underpants.

"What are you going to do to me, Mom?" I asked with tremendous effort to find my voice.

I was overcome with desperation that almost prevented me from speaking or moving to ask that simple but important question. I glanced sideways, waiting to see if my mother would go to the kitchen to heat a knife to red-hot again. But that didn't happen. The woman sang with her deep, raspy voice a strange melody in her language and smiled kindly at me, as if trying to let me know that this was the most natural thing in the world and I shouldn't worry. She knelt at my feet, opened my legs, took off my undergarment, and I felt her warm hand on my vagina. In less time than it takes a rooster to crow, I felt something cold run through my entire nervous system, an electric shock from my tailbone to my spinal cord, a brief but intense cut that compressed my pineal gland, causing my eyes to roll back, and after five seconds, it began to burn and gradually turned into an unbearable pain that ripped through my throat with my screams. Despite my body being in muscular and nervous shock, I tried to wriggle away, but the woman held my legs and kept singing while my mother exerted all her strength, pressing her weight against my shoulders and shouting:

"Stay still and be quiet, Andrea, be quiet or it'll be worse!"

I could barely maintain consciousness, my eyes half-open. My mind urgently tried to disconnect, to do something to alleviate the pain, while perhaps other forces wanted me to remain alert so as not to bleed out. With a Gillette razor, the healer swiftly and permanently removed what made me a woman. My mother took my bloodied clitoris with her fingers and, with a savage gaze, told me, "You won't need this anymore because you're getting married." I will never forget her laughter as she walked away to throw a part of my feminine essence in the trash. The native woman, very calm, helped me sit in the bath with water and salt, and she placed a blanket on my back while continuing to sing to me. My mother paid her, and the woman left. I didn't know where María Eugenia went after the gruesome mutilation of my body. I stayed there, crying with a tormented soul, watching in astonishment as my tears fell and disappeared into the red, salty water. I bled for at least an hour. My legs fell asleep, and it seemed impossible to stand up, but I managed. I covered my vagina with a towel and walked in a dying state to my room, where I lay down. Then, the few remaining colors of life vanished with my sleep and weakness.

Female genital mutilation is a horrific and unthinkable act for the majority of societies outside of Africa, the Middle East, and Asia. However, for many tribes and religious clans, it is a sociocultural duty that has been carried out for thousands of years. Among the reasons cited by those who practice and defend this assault on the sexuality and dignity of young girls are concepts of purity, tradition, religion, and the backward belief or conviction that women were created solely for procreation and to be faithful to their husbands, not for desire or sexual pleasure. Most victims don't even know that they have been victimized, and it is difficult for them to understand because their sisters, mothers, grandmothers, aunts, and all their female ancestors have gone through the same, including this woman who has mutilated me. Therefore, it is a social duty they must accept in order to marry and start a family. If they refuse, women are excluded, expelled, and discriminated against in villages and tribes, and it is a punishment they will carry for their entire lives, a personal stigma that can make the rest of their days a greater misery than not having a clitoris. This practice takes place every day in these corners of the world where girls like me are directly exposed to death, hemorrhages, infections, traumas, pains, and irreversible chronic consequences of genital mutilation.

For my mother, who had acquired this cultural knowledge, it was something that I had to fulfill as part of the agreement to be married off. My only consolation is to hope that one day education can be the force that brings about these changes and ends this human aberration forever. Unfortunately, as I mentioned before, the imagination of humans knows no limits, and it is closely tied to beliefs and customs that are passed down from generation to generation until they manifest as almost absolute truths. Despite everything and my own tragedy, the "civilized" world cannot point fingers at Africa while, for example, in Myanmar, women have their faces tattooed to make them appear less attractive because, according to tradition, Chinese men would abduct girls for their beauty. Or in India, babies are dropped from the tops of temples in free fall to be caught in stretched cloths held by their parents, which is believed to bring prosperity, strength, and luck, according to popular belief.

The Catholic Church itself allows self-flagellation through whip lashes on the back, sometimes even causing layers of skin to be lost, not to mention the customary horrors of the Inquisition, the punishments inflicted by missionaries on indigenous peoples, or the sexual abuse of minors by depraved priests cannot be ignored. How can we not mention, on the same level, Jews living in a "more modern and educated" world who practice male circumcision on babies, where, to make this tradition even more peculiar, the rabbi performing the ceremony sucks the baby's penis with his mouth to stop the bleeding, causing the baby to cry out in agony? Or the ultra-Orthodox Jews in Brooklyn who beat each other with innocent live chickens to atone for their sins and force their women to be bald and wear wigs, similar to African customs, to avoid attracting other men. Thousands of years ago in Mexico, the Aztecs and Mayans would roll heads downhill from their pyramids, and until a century ago, the Chinese would break and bind the fingers of young girls to stunt their growth and achieve smaller feet, which were considered beautiful. In Rome, families would enjoy their weekends watching as lions, bears, or tigers tore prisoners apart in the coliseums. In Bolivia, they tie condors to the back of a bull, and the condor pecks at the bull's neck while the bull shakes and gores the condor in a horrific act devoid of any compassion. All around the world, even the most bizarre religious traditions and festivities are practiced, always at the expense of a victim, be it a woman, a child, or an animal. These are different beliefs and traditions that ultimately go against the effort of nature to evolve in a coherent, wise, and rational manner. I have been a victim of these beliefs, of history, and of what my mother absurdly conceived in her distorted mind.

Since then, my life changed radically. I stopped smiling, even with Ruby. The pain from my genital mutilation was unbearable, a hurt rooted in the essence of female humanity. I spent long sleepless nights, fearing that I would accidentally reopen the wound that, at an agonizingly slow pace, refused to heal. Going to the bathroom was a separate torture. Sometimes, in the silence of the night, I felt pains that forced me to cry, and I would cover my face and mouth with the pillow so that my mother wouldn't hear me. I had to carefully tend to and protect my wound to avoid any infection, and as soon as it healed, I would resume my plan to end my own life.

Before the husband chosen by my mother came for me, and if that wasn't possible, I had to spend my sleepless minutes planning something else. A month and a half passed, and I escaped the danger. I would cut pieces of fabric and fold them to protect my wound, and with that, I was able to return to school, making an effort to walk normally and conceal all my discomfort.

The Master Plan

After a long time, I was able to see my friend Alexandra again, who was the only solace I had after going through that torture and the only one who knew about it. She gave me hope and helped me think of impossible ways to escape or get through it. During those days, still in recovery, I started experiencing sharp pains in my abdomen, which caused me great concern, and I didn't know what to do.

One afternoon, when I returned from school, I immediately changed my cloths, which I washed by hand to reuse, only to discover to my panic that they were stained with blood. Once again, the shadows of the night enveloped me with terrifying thoughts, and I thought that as soon as I fell asleep, I would bleed to death and pass into the world of light that I had once visited. I thought this was the perfect opportunity to leave this world and managed to relax and fall asleep, hoping to never wake up. But Ruby's barking and the first rays of sunlight that entered through the curtains in my room played a trick on me. As I opened my eyes, I realized, to my misfortune, that I was still alive, but the worst part was that the bleeding hadn't stopped. I went to school carrying some extra cloths in my bag to change, in case I didn't die in the attempt.

Alexandra listened attentively and said that we should tell her mom after school. As we left, she took me by the hand, and we walked towards her mother, who was waiting by the school gate. When she saw me, she was surprised by my panicked face and paleness and offered me water.

"What's wrong, my child? Where does it hurt?" said the kind woman, her white robe wrapped around her shaved head, as she stroked my cheek and checked my temperature with her hand on my forehead.

"Tell me, what's happening?" she asked with concern in her deep and gentle voice.

"A few days ago, I started experiencing strong pains in my abdomen, and yesterday I began to bleed. Last month, my mother had someone come to castrate me, and I'm afraid that the wound is infected or open," I said, my chin trembling, on the verge of tears.

She checked my eyes, ears, and tongue, and took my temperature again. Then, with confidence and tenderness in her words and gaze, she said, "Don't worry, my child. You're becoming a young woman. From now on, this will happen to you every month for many years. Don't be scared, it's normal."

I could feel her motherly warmth as she placed my hands between hers to comfort me. And then, cautiously and discreetly, the three of us walked to the man who sold juices across the street, and she bought pineapple and mango juice for me and her daughter. They accompanied me a little further on my way back home while she talked to me about women's cycles and female sexuality. I gave her a kiss on the cheek and said goodbye to Alexandra, thinking that my plan to die from internal bleeding would no longer work, so I urgently needed to find an alternative.

Around that time, my mother started experiencing different ailments. One day she had a headache, the next day it was her waist, and the following day it was her knees. On that day, she went to work and came home early. As usual, she entered without greeting anyone, except for a glance at her plants, which were the only things she lavished her love and dedication on, aside from her work and expeditions. She went straight to her room and called me with less vocal rigidity than before.

"Andrea Fabi, prepare me some tea," she said.

"I'll bring it to you right away, Mom," I replied.

With the cup of tea in my hand, and with great concentration to avoid any accident that could cost me dearly, I walked to her dimly lit room. I stretched my leg and pushed the door open with my foot just as she turned on her carved ivory lamp with the red shade. The one that cast a crimson hue over her nightly escapades.

She looked very tired, dressed in all black, and took off her white and red bracelets. She had let her hair down, and that, coupled with her half-inch of eyeliner, made her appear even more imposing, causing my skin to crawl.

"Leave my tea here and pass me the bag that's on the chair." I turned around and picked up her bag which smelled like cigarettes, smoke, sex, leather, sins, and perfume. She received it and started searching inside. She took out her wallet, checked it, and continued searching.

"I thought I had money in here... Andrea, on the shelf in the living room, there's a gray and brown book with a picture of two feathered shamans. Inside, I have some money. If it's not there, look in the red book with gold letters. Take a $20 bill and run to the pharmacy to buy me Valium. I don't want you to be late or get distracted, understood?"

"Yes, Mom, I'll go right away," I replied in a low voice.

I hurried to the living room and stood in front of the bookshelf. It took me no more than two seconds to find the one María Eugenia had mentioned. I opened it and flicked through the pages with my thumb. I found money and took just enough, while out of the corner of my eye, in slow motion like an autumn leaf, I saw a small piece of paper gently falling to the ground, defying gravity. I bent down, picked it up, unfolded it, and read. My breath stopped. I swallowed saliva and turned my head towards the hallway to my mother's room to ensure she was still in bed. With the stealth of a feral cat, I slid into the kitchen to find another piece of paper and copied an address, a phone number, and a written name: Samuel Armstrong.

As I wrote, I made sure to breathe as silently as possible so that my ears could detect my mother's footsteps at any moment. The truth is, I'm not even sure if I was breathing. I folded the paper back exactly as it was and put it in the book, returning it to its place, but my arm remained extended and my hand wouldn't let go when a whisper in my mind told me, "*Take more money because you'll need it to call and escape.*" I risked my life a few more times to take out a couple more bills. I regretted it and put them back, but then I took them out again, repeating this a couple more times until finally I bravely decided to keep them for a just cause, which wasn't the same as stealing. I set off towards the pharmacy, running as fast as I could to save time so I could use whatever spare moments I had to call my father. I forgot my pains, my sadness, and my planned suicide. Everything came back to life, I could distinguish colors again, smell and hear the sea, and somehow I knew that those beings of light I had seen on my path to death wanted to protect me. That's why, by giving me smiles, they had denied me the stay in their illuminated world. They never told me where my father was because they knew that my path to freedom was in the real world.

I looked up and saw a seagull crossing the sky between two buildings, and I thought, '*That's me, one building is my past and the other is my future, I just have to fly.*' I entered the pharmacy, bowing my head, and bought the medicine. Then I started walking towards the city center, where there was a call center a few blocks away. I preferred to walk instead of run to avoid drawing attention and prevent someone from recognizing me and informing my mother. Every few businesses and bazaars, I would enter and from inside, I would glance to make sure no one was following me, pretending at the same time that I was interested in buying something. I managed to reach the call center, and upon entering, I recognized a neighbor who was paying. I left and entered the adjacent watch store until I saw him leave. My heart was pounding, almost about to jump out of my chest. I exchanged coins with the young man behind the counter, who assigned me a booth. I inserted the coins and dialed the number. The phone made every attempt to connect with its counterpart on the other side of the world, but I could only hear someone speaking in English and then a beep, after which I hung up, unsure of what to do. I tried two more times without success.

What should I do? Should I go back home with the medicine or keep trying? Panic started to completely take over, and the world turned gray again as I decided to run back home. Before reaching there, I stopped and hid the paper inside my shoe, feeling stabs and pains from the rush. I stealthily peeked through the gate to see if my mother was preparing a new deadly ambush. This time, I had an idea, a plan, an escape, a hope. The gods were on my side, so if she were to attack me, I would flee from my executioner at all costs. But she wasn't there in the yard. I entered and made an effort to calm my breathing before going to her room. I poured a glass of water and then took it to her. She was asleep. I left the pills, the water, and quietly closed her door without making a sound.

I couldn't stop thinking about that paper with my father's name and phone number. Eugenia hid it in a book she wrote and published, *The Wise Voices of Ifa*. Yes, the same one who named me Fabi. I don't know if Ifa was truly wise or not, but at least it gave me hope tucked away within its words. My mother had met the king of a Nigerian tribe, who, in honor of their friendship, gave her his personally carved mahogany walking pole, which she cherished and kept beside her bed. On the cover of the book, the self-righteous man appeared alongside his son and the staff, in a photograph my mother herself captured during her tribal research visit.

My mother had a rotary phone at home, but she put a lock on it, preventing me from making calls, just like her room, which she locked when she was away. Suddenly, I remembered that the neighbor had a telephone! I waited until the next day when my mother took her nap and hurriedly ran to the neighbor, who kindly let me use the phone without asking any questions. I was about to give up when I heard that deep, kind voice speaking a message in English that I didn't understand. Then, the beep sounded, and by pure instinct, I knew I had to leave a voice message. I tried to muster my limited English, but the excitement allowed me to think only in French:

"I would like to speak with Samuel Armstrong, please. My name is Andrea, and I am his daughter. I'm calling to let him know that my life is in danger, and I need someone to help me. My mother is a criminal and has abused me for years. She has sold me to someone from a tribe who will come looking for me soon. Please, I need help. Father, if you hear this message, don't call my mother or the police because they are corrupted by her. I will call again tomorrow, around the same time. Goodbye."

The next day, I waited again for my mother to take her sleeping pill and fall asleep, and then I raced to the neighbor's house, who kindly let me use the phone once more. Samuel Armstrong waited patiently, concerned, and very emotional. He had heard the message I left, pulled up a chair, grabbed a few books, and stayed by the phone without moving for many hours until it rang again.

"Andrea, daughter, is it you?" he said to me, his French still intact and with a tone of concern. Upon hearing his voice, the world started spinning again, the sky turned blue, and my heartbeat with love.

"Hello, Dad!" I said, my voice on the brink of bursting into tears.

"I don't have much time to explain, but my life is in danger, and I need your help, please Father, it's urgent. My mother has done terrible things to me, and I need you to get me out of here as soon as possible! She's insane. This morning, I overheard her talking to someone about sewing my vagina shut to prepare me for marriage... she's sold me, and I don't know what to do."

"Yes, daughter! I'll do whatever I can to help you. I have a friend in Dakar whom you can reach out to in case of an emergency. Do you have a pen nearby to write down her number?"

"Yes, Father, I've written it down. Dad, listen to me, I never wrote that letter. She forced me to do it at gunpoint. Please, help me, Dad!"

"I believe you, daughter, I believe you. If anything happens, go to the United States embassy. Call me back in three days, and I'll have a plan to help you, okay? Take good care of yourself. I love you, daughter!"

"I'll call you in three days. Thank you, Dad. I love you!"

My heart couldn't contain its own happiness, which I had to conceal at all costs, until the call. I thought my father, after all these years, would be another person to turn his back on me and believe that I was the crazy one. But he had already experienced every existential crisis of María Eugenia's and immediately believed each and every one of my words. Furthermore, I sensed desperation in his voice, and I knew he wouldn't disappoint me. Meanwhile, to my misfortune, my mother started feeling better, and I would see her going out to the courtyard to water her plants. I did everything humanly possible to avoid drawing her attention because the more she ignored me, the better my chances of escape took shape. On the third day, she didn't take her afternoon nap or lie down due to any discomfort, but before sunset, she perfumed herself, got into her car, and went off, perhaps for some espionage mission or to visit one of her lovers, accompanied by her purse overflowing with saints, cigarettes, makeup, jewelry, and whatever else you can imagine.

As soon as I saw her turning the corner, leaving behind a trail of suspended orange dust pierced by the last rays of the sun, I ran to my neighbor's house. Upon seeing me arrive, she placed the telephone by the window, ready for me to use it, but not before warning me in an authoritative voice that she would start charging me for the following calls. I reassured her, saying not to worry, that I had some money and would pay her without any problems. One by one, I dialed the numbers on the holes of the rotary dial, spinning them and then releasing them as the dial returned to its position, ready for the next number. As I did this, my mind only wanted to hear my father's voice saying, "I had her arrested. You can relax."

When I finished dialing, it only took a couple of seconds for someone to answer. On the other side of the Atlantic, a woman with a very rigid accent spoke to me. Monika was my father's German wife, and we both made our best efforts to communicate as she told me:

"Your dad is there, he just arrived at Hotel Nina. I just spoke with him."

The only thing I could understand was "Hotel Nina."

"Mon père est à l'hôtel Nina?" (Is my father at Hotel Nina?) I asked desperately, trying to break the language barrier.

"Oui, oui, merci, merci! Hotel Nina!"

I couldn't contain my excitement without having a heart attack right then and there. I hung up the phone and paused for a few seconds to plan my next move. This was the master plan, and any mistake would be fatal. I could either stay home or risk taking the bus and going to the hotel in the city center, possibly running into my mother at any moment. The decision was made. It was now or never.

I couldn't believe that my father was already setting foot on African soil after just three days, I had to confirm it as soon as possible. I ran to the coastal avenue and boarded the first bus that came. I discreetly sank into my seat, making sure no one noticed I was there. I anxiously peered out the window to make sure my mother's car wasn't following the bus. I did the same when I got off, looking around in a panic, searching for the orange Beetle. Just one block away from where the bus dropped me off, that hotel stood, and I walked down the street towards it.

I had been there many times before, so I didn't need any directions to get there. It was a brown building of moderate height with a modern architecture that resembled an accordion, with many windows and air conditioning units. I rushed into the reception area, hoping to see my father sitting in one of the waiting chairs, but there was only the receptionist behind the counter, reading a magazine and paying no attention to me. I approached him and asked for Samuel Armstrong. He checked his registration book and quickly told me:

"Is he the American gentleman with a beard?"

"Oui, oui, oui!" I replied.

"He left for dinner about ten minutes ago. If you want, you can wait for him, or I can leave him a message for you." So, I asked him for some paper and a pencil and wrote in French:

"Thursday, September 15th, 1988. Dad, I came to the hotel, but you weren't here. I called your wife in the United States, and she told me you were in Senegal, so I came right away. I waited for you here until 8:30. I had to go home, or Mom will worry. If she sends me somewhere or asks me to run an errand, I'll come as soon as I can tomorrow, but I don't know what time. Please wait for me. I love you. Andrea."

I left the note with the receptionist and hurried back home. Thank you to Ifa or the beings of light who granted me the joy of returning to my home while María Eugenia was still out. I tidied up a bit, washed the dishes, and left everything clean and organized before going to bed. That night, I could hardly close an eye. I wondered if my father would recognize me or if I would recognize him. A thousand thoughts of events that never happened crossed my mind, and sometimes I was overwhelmed with fear at the thought of my mother discovering something or someone blowing the news that they saw me or my father in the city center. If she finds out he's here, she will not only send the police but also the Senegalese army to arrest him and make him disappear into the sea or underground, just like Pinochet style. And beyond my somewhat negative thoughts, I had the intuition that my father was also very worried and scared to death of being discovered. He was also a well-known man in the region, and despite the years that had passed, there was a great possibility that someone would recognize him. I remember that, before falling asleep in the early morning, my mother still hadn't come home.

When the sun started to rise, I jumped out of bed and the first thing I did was to go and check if the Beetle was on the street. There it was, the Bug. I suppose it arrived at dawn, but I didn't hear it. I washed my face and got ready for school as I did every day. But this time, I didn't take my notebooks. Instead, I hid them under the bed. I emptied my school bag and put some clothes, some photos, and an ABBA cassette tape, one by Julio Iglesias and another one by Kenny Rogers, which I liked because it reminded me of my father. I quietly closed the door and went out into the patio. Ruby was lying on the ground and looking at me with a sad and indifferent gaze, as if she knew in advance that this was a farewell. I caressed her, kissed her, held back my tears, and ran to catch the bus. As I left the house, I saw the neighbor and waved goodbye, but before I could continue, I turned back to her with an improvised but urgent lie:

"Neighbor, I have a friend who had an accident and is in the hospital, and I will visit her after school. My mother is asleep, and if she asks about me when she wakes up and I haven't returned, please tell her that I'm at the hospital."

With that desperate ruse, I intended to buy time and also distract my mother if she went looking for me if I didn't come back after school. At exactly 8 o'clock in the morning, I was standing outside Hotel Nina. I opened the main door and entered through the central lobby. Many people were coming and going from the building at that hour, including tourists and passing traders. I noticed that there were now two receptionists, both busy attending to customers. Suddenly, the elevator bell rang, and at the same time, the number 1 appeared on the black display with green numbers, like the calculators of that time. The door opened, and then I saw this big, strong man whom I immediately recognized by his beard. After looking at the watch on his wrist, he looked up, and our eyes met. We smiled simultaneously and ran towards each other to embrace. It was a long, silent, almost eternal hug. I felt his warmth, his scent, his sincerity, and his concern. He felt my coldness, my fear, my fragility. Very excited, he took me in his arms, and I felt like I was embraced by a freshly arrived Grizzly bear from Alaska lifting me out of the water like a salmon swimming upstream. We cried as we looked at each other, trying to recognize one another. I was no longer the baby in diapers that he still held in his memory, and all his hair had turned white, including his beard. He took my hands and looked into my eyes, as if saying over and over again, "I'm here, daughter. I've come back for you."

But the words wouldn't come out. He wiped his eyes and with a wide smile asked me, "Have you had breakfast, daughter?"

"Not yet Dad. I left home and came straight to the hotel. My mother has been deeply asleep since she arrived at dawn. She won't wake up until 2 p.m."

He took my bag, held my hand, and we went to the dining area to have breakfast. We sat at the last table, farthest from the buffet and the people. Between him and me, there was a cruet with salt, pepper, oil, hot sauce, small cups of jam, butter, and a jar of sugar. There was a chrome napkin holder and a menu stand on the side. He pushed everything to the side of the table, and we held hands.

"Tell me, how are you, Andrea? Are you doing well in school?"

"To be honest, despite everything I have to endure, I try to do what I can in school. I have good grades. But sometimes I have to be absent for long periods of time when my mother punishes me. My mother is crazy, Dad... Please help me and get me out of here! But I warn you, you must be careful because she has powerful contacts in the city."

At that moment, I thought of all the stories my mind had imagined about this reunion, and some of them included this moment when my father would tell me that he would go to the police to report her. And if that was his plan, I had to prevent it at all costs because it put both of us at risk. I told him many things in a low voice while every couple of minutes, my father handed me a new napkin to blow my nose and wipe my tears.

"I know your mother very well, daughter, and I know perfectly well what she's capable of. I distanced myself from her for that very reason and for my own mental health. The early years were beautiful when we traveled the world, but it didn't take long for it to become a nightmare. When I left, I knew that fighting for custody or taking you with me would be a lost cause because she would never allow it. Maybe without me by her side and having you as a responsibility, I thought she would figure out her internal conflicts and better control her strange personality. Forgive me, daughter, I never thought it would make it even worse. But I'm here to help you and for us to reunite and never separate again. Let's go to my room to pick up my suitcase and documents, and then we'll find shelter, don't worry."

We finished breakfast, he went to pay for what we consumed, and we went up to his room, I remember it well, 307. It was my first time in an elevator. He let me press the floor number, and as we ascended, I hugged him and felt safer and happier than ever. He told me that our phone call was one of the most beautiful but also the most worrisome moments of his life. He felt the same excitement as when he saw me being born, and as soon as we finished talking, he got in his car and went to a travel agency in Hollister to buy his plane ticket. He had slept very little in the past few days. Apparently, he only lay on the bed last night as everything was in order with his briefcase on the chair. He went to the bathroom, and then we got ready to leave. We reached the reception area and stopped.

"Wait for me here, daughter. I'll go out to the street and hail a taxi. Don't leave until I tell you."

Watching him through the windows of the building, I waited until he hailed a taxi and then looked around, opened the door, and signaled me. I ran and we got into the car, he closed the door, and held my hand.

"To the United States Embassy, please, my friend."

He gave me a smile and then looked away to observe the streets of Dakar.

"It hasn't changed much," he said while he carefully observed everything, as if searching for the past he had left in that city many years ago. He followed people with his gaze, and a slight smile appeared on his face, as if remembering friends, experiences, his work, and his travels through these lands. Since Sam returned to the United States in love with Monika, he had stopped roaming the planet and settled in Hollister, a city less than two hours south of San Francisco in California, isolated from the hustle and bustle of larger cities like San Jose and Oakland. He had spent the last few years providing consultations and some classes. At that moment, inside the taxi, I knew that all those nights dreaming of a better life were about to become a reality. I knew that this man hadn't forgotten me, in fact, he always had me in his mind and his heart, and I could perceive it in his words, his gaze, and his concern for me. By that time in the morning, the sun was casting its rays over the city, and a gentle sea breeze made everything flow harmoniously among the crowd and the vehicles. I opened the window slightly, took a deep breath, closed my eyes, and felt that everything would be alright by my father's side, while squeezing his hand and both of us feeling a strange chill on our skin, perhaps stemming from the fear of being detected by the police, my mother, or someone who might recognize us. We had to be very cautious, and as a precaution, we remained silent inside the car, which stopped in front of the imposing building after about fifteen minutes of driving.

My generous father brought a smile to the driver's face when he paid him, while also asking him not to mention our brief trip to the Embassy to anyone, to which the man kindly nodded. We hurriedly got out and walked quickly towards the entrance.

The World of Ronald

There are very exciting moments in life, and this was one of them. We were just a few steps away from those massive walls and windows that could provide us with the only protection we would find in this country. Each second manifested itself in parallel with a pounding in our chests completely beyond anyone's control and will, and it was also reflected in our faces, stressed by fear and anxiety. All we could do was offer a false calmness so as not to draw more attention than necessary. Suddenly, we were inside the building, and both our hearts could rest, allowing our lungs to expand again after a mutual sigh that brought forth an inexplicable simultaneous laughter, so liberating that I will never forget it. A younger officer, but as tall as my father, asked him about his visit, to which he presented his passport and replied:

"I'm an American citizen and this is my daughter who is in danger, and we both need immediate protection."

The only word I understood was "protection", which made it clear to me that somehow, we would be safe within that sturdy cement cube. After passing through metal detectors and emptying our few belongings, we were led to a lobby where we waited for about twenty more minutes until a formally dressed lady arrived and greeted my father politely.

"Nice to meet you, Mr. Armstrong. I am Officer Ann Sides. How may I help you?"

My father stood up from his chair, extended his hand with a wide smile, ran his hand through his hair, and then both of them moved further away from me, walking slowly. They engaged in a low conversation while the woman glanced at me and smiled every time our eyes met, which helped calm my nerves from a distance. She told my father to follow her to her office and indicated that we could leave our belongings in custody. As we entered her workplace, the first thing I saw was a large photograph in the middle of the wall of a man with a warm smile and a red tie, posing in front of the American flag, impeccably dressed with a white handkerchief in the pocket of his jacket. At the bottom of the frame, there was an engraving on a bronze plaque that said Ronald Reagan, 40th President of the USA.

After a moment, another man entered the office and took my father's passport. The woman asked Sam many questions, then picked up the phone, which was made of black and shiny bakelite, just like my neighbor's phone, and spoke for a few minutes with someone while drawing unintentional little flowers, circles, cubes, and stars on a piece of paper. Every now and then, she turned to look at me and winked with a friendly smile. My father rubbed his hands together and looked out through the window. After half an hour of the interview, a uniformed man with a weapon at his waist entered the room and placed some documents on the desk, which the officer began to read attentively. My father would suddenly look at me and offer me half-smiles, very nervous. Then, just like Agent Sides, he would wink at me. When I looked back at the man in the photo on the wall, I imagined that he was also winking at me to confirm that what my father was doing was right. And since María Eugenia was friends with the president of Senegal, I didn't rule out the possibility that Reagan and my father were also friends and that he might appear at any moment through the door.

Ann Sides began to review the documents brought by the armed officer and read in astonishment an internal report from the Senegalese police stating that recently, Mrs. María Eugenia Castillo García Huidobro had been arrested for kidnapping, extortion, and sexual assault on a diplomat from Mauritania, and possession of an unregistered weapon in the country. She stood up and approached me, examining the scar around my eye in detail, and then asked permission to see the scar on my head. She made me open my mouth and saw some broken teeth, checked my hands, legs, and back, which also showed scars of all styles, sizes, and shapes. She noted down everything she observed in a notebook. She made my father fill out another document that obliged him to take me for an urgent medical examination and a psychological interview with a professional. Then she asked us to follow her, and we walked to another office where more people were working at their desks.

There was Ann Sides, with her impeccable blue suit and heels, her USA flag pin, her straight hair tied back, one arm supporting the folder with documents and the other extended like a clock pendulum, swinging perfectly, while in her hand, she spun her silver metal pencil with her fingers, all in perfect rhythm with her confident and solid hips walking ahead of us. She introduced us to another lady who received her folder and immediately started typing on her typewriter while multitasking, reading, asking questions to my father, and then asking me questions that he translated from English to French. She asked me for my date of birth, where I lived, the names of my mother and father, and if I had any more family in Senegal, to which I said no, except for Ruby and the other Sam, the chameleon.

Once she finished her interview and her rhythmic relationship with the noisy typewriter, she asked me to stand in front of a small retractable screen of light blue color and look straight into the camera. Then she took a photograph of me. Immediately after, she asked us to follow her back to Officer Sides' office. That lady, along with Ronald, my father's friend, welcomed us again with a smile.

"Take a seat. Would you like something to drink?" she asked.

"Just water, please," my father replied.

I asked for a Coca-Cola to start getting accustomed to this Americanized environment.

"Of course, wait for me here, I'll be right back," said the woman.

We were left alone in silence. My father broke the silence by pointing his finger at his comrade:

"He is the President of the United States, his name is Ronald Reagan. He was a famous Hollywood actor. Have you heard of Hollywood, where movies are filmed? I'll take you to visit those places, my love."

With her characteristically firm, synchronized, and decisive steps, this woman stood beside Sam and placed a passport with my photo glued inside on the desk in front of him. Then she signed and stamped the document with authority and feminine power and said to me, "Have a good trip back home, sweety," while giving me the Coca-Cola with a smile from ear to ear. Samuel jumped out of his chair, brushed his hair to one side, and took the agent's hands with both of his, thanking her for all her efforts, to which the woman responded by giving him a platonic hug and another one to me, saying, "Goodbye Andrea."

We walked back down the hallway, and as we reached the large main hall, I turned my head and saw Officer Sides still far in the distance, waving goodbye to me with a sweeping motion of her hand. Then we entered another room where we had to wait for at least an hour until a well-dressed man arrived and handed my father two plane tickets. He showed us where the buffet dining area was for lunch and the lounges to freshen up, and he also showed us a cozy private room with comfortable armchairs, a television, a small kitchen with a fully stocked refrigerator and more Coca-Cola. We went to have lunch, and my father cleverly took the opportunity to make me laugh by sharing his adventures and anecdotes from around the world, stories about his family in New Hampshire, New York, and Hollister, and how he managed to get here so quickly, all instead of ruining our meal by asking me to talk about my own life. We saved that for later when we went to the living room. We were two refugees within the embassy, waiting for the moment when we had to go through the guillotine: airport immigration control.

When we went to rest in the living room, I had enough time to pour out my heart to my father and tell him about all my tragedies, one by one. We cried together, and every now and then, he would apologize for abandoning me, to which I assured him that I fully understood his reasons for separating from my mother. He told me how he bit his tongue and wiped away his tears when he read that letter where I blamed him for everything and insulted him, unaware that every word was coerced. He reminded me of Baba and other animals, my childhood friends, and brought back memories of the images and names of those women who took care of me so devotedly when I was a child, reviving the time when the three of us were happy, something that I had forgotten amidst all the suffering. At the same time, I shared with him about Alexandra and her mom, who were among the few people who lent me a helping hand. I confessed about my intimate wounds, told him that I had started growing pubic hair but not in the affected place where my mother and her demonic dragons cauterized me with a red-hot knife.

"You know my grandparents, right, Dad?"

"Of course, my daughter. Your grandfather, Sergio, is a great man, a very important military figure in Chile, and your grandmother is a refined and affectionate woman whom I held in great respect."

"But my mother never told you what her father did to her?"

"No, what do you mean? What did he do?"

"The same thing that Professor Abdou did to me."

"What are you saying, daughter? Don't say that, it can't be true!"

"I saw them with my own eyes, Dad. I saw them at least three times, and I overheard them on other occasions. And my poor grandmother, I'm certain she knew, I was about to tell her, but I was so scared of that man and my mother."

Sam looked down, searching for explanations. He clenched his fists and shook his head in denial. After a long pause, he continued.

"Now things start to make sense, my daughter. I can begin to understand your mother's demons. How did I not realize? It's madness. Now that you mention it, I remember some strange behavior from her when we were in Brazil and your grandmother came to visit. It's as if the lady wanted to tell me something, but her voice was muted, or Eugenia always had an excuse to keep her away from me. Many little details, insinuations and strange moments come to mind when your grandfather visited us."

Suddenly, without us realizing that dusk was approaching, someone knocked on the door, and my father told them to come in.

"It's time, Mr. Armstrong. The taxi is waiting for you. I'll accompany you to the exit."

In funeral silence, we walked down the illuminated corridor to the exit, where, in my terrified imagination, I could clearly see Eugenia herself waiting for us on the street, guarded by the Senegalese army, and right behind her, the taxi driver gagged with the vehicle engulfed in flames. But those panic-induced thoughts of not making it to the plane deceived me because there was a friendly taxi driver with his cigarette and beret, ready to help us with our bags with attentive eagerness.

"Thank you very much for everything," my father said, shaking hands with the embassy agent.

"You know, Mr. Armstrong, we'll be keeping a close eye on things, this is your home," the man replied before getting us into the vehicle.

"You guys are American tourists?" the taxi driver asked, turning his head towards the back seat with an overly stretched smile.

"Yes, my friend, just tourists. We're going back home."

"Ok, ok, you guys like Senegalese music?"

"Yes, yes," I responded in my limited English.

Without any rush, the man took his time to find his favorite cassette and inserted it into the mouth of the stereo, which swallowed it to make our journey to the airport a less stressful moment than we expected. In fact, it was fun. While my father got distracted watching the sea and the fishermen casting their nets from their long boats, I entertained myself by looking at the myriad of decorations inside the taxi, from images of saints to mirrors, family photographs, toys, necklaces, animal teeth, feathers, and his collection of cassettes in a hand-polished wooden box, among other things. The trip felt short, and before we knew it, we were already outside the Leopold Sedar Senghor International Airport.

"Papa, do you know who owns this airport?"

"If you are asking because it's the president's name, I've met him personally, but he's not the owner!"

"He's very friendly with my mom; he does her many favors."

"I don't doubt it, daughter..."

Discreetly, without the driver noticing, my father signaled for me to stay in the seat for a moment. He got out, adjusting his hat and beard, scanning the area with a gaze like a coastal lighthouse searching for sailors in the fog. He observed the people slowly, making sure we were not in danger. Then he turned around and opened the door for me. He paid the man, thanked him for his service, took my belongings, his suitcase, and firmly held my hand, leading me inside the airport. My heart was racing, and I could clearly sense the tension and nervousness in Sam. Additionally, I couldn't stop thinking about how furious my mother must have been when she didn't see me coming home from school. She must have gone to look for me, and they must have told her that I wasn't there, so she'd surely resort to using all her connections to ask about me. Suddenly, I remembered the neighbor and prayed that my mother and her furious dragons were wandering around the hospital where I was supposed to be. We started walking towards the immigration and international police counter, and I'm sure those were the longest minutes of our lives.

"Don't say anything, daughter. Let me do the talking, and you just smile, okay?" my father whispered to me.

We stood in front of this uniformed man, black as night, the whites of his eyes contrasting against his skin. My father handed him his passport and mine, freshly baked and smelling new. The officer asked about my mother, to which Samuel, leaning closer, quietly said, "she passed away recently," putting his finger to his lips, signaling silence so that I wouldn't hear and the officer wouldn't make me cry with such an untimely and thoughtless question.

"I'm very sorry, Mr. Armstrong," the officer responded, taking the passports and stamping them with an exit mark. "Have a safe journey."

Without any expression on our faces, containing our nerves and happiness, we approached the boarding area, and after twenty tense minutes of not speaking and ready to run anywhere at any second, the doors opened for us to walk across the tarmac to the airplane. As we walked on the pavement, we discreetly looked back one last time to make sure that María Eugenia and her dragons, President Leopold, Tata Isabel, the Mauritanian camel, the corrupt police officers, the soldiers, and half of Senegal weren't running after us. We climbed the mobile stairs by the side of the plane and quickly located our seats. Even when we were settled, we still anxiously looked out the window, expecting to see my mother followed by a hundred Senegalese police cars arresting the flying machine. Finally, the door closed. The flight attendants began delivering their safety and evacuation instructions, which felt like an endless theater performance at the moment. Suddenly, the airplane began to move, positioned itself, and accelerated until it lifted off the ground. As soon as it did, my father embraced me, and we exhaled, sighed, and smiled through tears of excitement, suppressing the urge to scream with joy and deafen all the passengers.

I peered out of the window to say goodbye to my beloved Africa, observing Dakar as it embraced the fading sunlight, while the city lights began to twinkle and illuminate the surroundings. The sea shimmered like a bed of golden sequins, and the buildings and streets displayed hues of copper and orange, with shadows gradually claiming corners of the city and the fields. Down below remained my suffering and years of silence and chronic abuse. I watched as that place, which witnessed my birth and upbringing, faded away, and before me stretched the vast and liberating Atlantic Ocean, welcoming me to my new life, like a blank page in a book inviting me to fill it with my long-suppressed truth. Down there, the night would soon embrace Eugenia's madness, and her demons would blame her for letting the favorite victim escape. I wondered if this would be the final chapter, a fresh start from here on. What would happen to my nightmares? What will I do with my memories and the profound sorrow of never seeing my animals again? How will I cope with the nostalgia of breathing the dust, brushing against the sand, and healing my skin in the sea? Will I ever see Alexandra and her mother again? Ruby? What will the United States be like?

As my mind oscillated between my past and my future, and this winged capsule traversed the space between the sky and the sea, suddenly, the flight attendant arrived, offering us dinner. We enjoyed our meal, and when my father fell asleep, I gazed at him intently. I observed the plane's interior, looked at the night's stars, and once again, I attentively observed my father. In the realm of my memories, the two cloth puppets, me and Superman as my savior, began to gently close that sad chapter of my life, transmuting those playful dreams into a vivid tapestry of palpable reality. In that moment, I discovered that the heroes I had seen in cartoon magazines truly existed, and I had one by my side. A real hero, exclusively for me.

New Life

We made a quick layover in Paris and then continued to America. We both woke up when everyone had finished their breakfast, and there was just over an hour left until we reached New York. I caught a glimpse of the Statue of Liberty through the window, although it appeared tiny, it represented the grandest thing I could hope for. My father began telling me about his family and all the people I would start to meet in my new country, starting with his father, who shared the same name. Grandfather Samuel, who had recently turned 88 years old, was eager to meet his African granddaughter. For some reason, I still felt a lot of fear and anxiety. I thought about my mother constantly, and I couldn't help but imagine her going mad, searching for me everywhere, with the police and military friends inspecting vehicles entering and leaving the city, looking for me in hotels and bars, intervening in the most dangerous and peripheral areas, asking neighbors, and surely shedding crocodile tears on the local radio, pleading with the community to join efforts in finding me. I even considered the possibility that María Eugenia might have linked my disappearance to an act of revenge by the wife of the kidnapped Mauritanian diplomat, and if that were the case, she would be willing to ignite a war between the two nations. Regardless of her intentions, I only hoped that my beloved Ruby would not suffer the consequences of all the recent events.

Above all, I wondered what would happen when that old man from the tribe arrived ready for the wedding. Would Eugenia return his money or shoot him in the forehead to make him stop bothering her and then bury him at sea? Would she dare to call or write to my father to tell him about the tragedy of my disappearance? A million questions and doubts haunted me, tightly packed in my backpack, without even mentioning them to Samuel. How would I communicate with my new family if I didn't speak English? What would happen at school? Would they make fun of me because of my African origins? All these uncertainties weighed heavily on my mind as we approached the beginning of our new life in America. Why am I African? Will they be racist towards me, even though I am as fair-skinned as the Gerber baby?

The plane landed, and contrary to the infinite colors of Dakar, everything on American soil was gray, cloudy, and dense. I couldn't see any bare land or dust, and the sea didn't sparkle like in Senegal. Everything was covered in concrete. The airport was huge and bustling. We approached the window, and without any issues, they let us pass, saying, "Welcome home."

We stepped out of the terminal, and the change was striking. The atmosphere was very different, everything was strikingly different, starting with the buildings that look like giants, cold and bored as the days go by. There were two buildings that were very large and identical. They called them the Twin Towers. I wondered if they were built at the same time, or if one was a copy because they liked how tall the first one turned out to be.

The taxis were big and spacious, but the drivers were apathetic and indifferent. They didn't even negotiate the price because there's a machine that calculates the miles or the time, and they make it run as soon as you get in. I know traffic in Senegal was chaotic, but it had rhythm, grace, and flowed magically. In contrast, this was so violent that it needed to be controlled by hundreds of regulations, laws, and police. It was a noisy city, with the incessant sounds of fire engines, police cars, or ambulances, amidst honking, music, conversations, a saxophonist, a boy selling newspapers, some strange languages that didn't seem like

English, and smells so different from what I was used to. I saw groups of young people with huge radios in the streets, dancing very differently from Senegalese people. They moved like electrified snakes and spun like spinning tops on the ground. I asked my father, and he told me it was a new trend called "breakdance". Every now and then, I saw a Michael Jackson impersonator dancing on street corners and in plazas. My father explained that they are just imitators because Michael Jackson is what's popular, they call him the "King of Pop".

"What's the name of that song playing?" I asked, very curious.

"It's called *Like a Virgin*, and the singer is Madonna. It's not a good song, my dear, don't pay attention to it," he replied.

I was struck by how frequently we passed by fast-food restaurants, coffee shops, and stores with colorful signs. The streets were filled with people, and everyone seems to be in a hurry. There was a constant buzz of activity, and it was overwhelming for me. I couldn't help but wonder how I would fit into this new world, with its fast pace and unfamiliar customs. Will I be accepted? Will I find my place? As we continued our journey through the city, I held onto the hope that I could carve out a new life for myself, embracing both my African roots and the opportunities that lay ahead in this new land.

I was greatly intrigued by the frequent signs on the road that said 'EXIT' and quietly pondered that perhaps those were the paths successful people take to pursue the American Dream, given that 'éxito' (success) in Spanish is similar to 'exit' in English." The taxi took us to Connecticut, to a perfect village with wide, clean streets, everything organized and in its place, just like in the movies. I was greatly impressed by the care given to the lawns, gardens, bushes, and trees surrounding the houses. Each one of them had an attached garage where people kept their vehicles. That was impressive. Back in Dakar, even owning a bicycle was a luxury, and if you had a place to store it, you were considered wealthy. My father was explaining many things about the country to me. Sometimes, he struggled to find the words in French, but after a few mime-like efforts, we managed to understand each other.

"You'll have to learn English, Andrea. That's the first thing," he said.

I remained silent while thinking that it would take me quite some time to feel at home. We arrived, and his entire family welcomed us. They were all eager to meet me, and for me, it was somewhat overwhelming because I could barely express myself due to the language barrier. However, their kindness overcame the situation, and for them, it was secondary issue. The happiest of them all was my grandfather Samuel. He looked at me intently, proudly took my hand, and was delighted to finally meet his granddaughter. He was a wise old man with the same kind gaze as my father. As soon as he received me, he began showing me some photos from when I was very young that his son used to send him from Africa, until one day they stopped coming. They prepared a room for me to sleep in, and tonight there will be a welcoming dinner. Susan and David, my father's nephews, are also curious to hear details about where I come from. They asked me if I had been around elephants, giraffes, and lions, and that makes me laugh. Little by little, the ice began to break around the unusual occasion of meeting the new Armstrong of the family. Susan asked me if I had clean clothes for dinner, and I, feeling a bit embarrassed, showed her the few rags I had in my backpack.

"Don't worry. Do you like going shopping?" she said.

I became nervous, thinking that she would make me put on a loose dress, empty my backpack, and get it ready to go look for free things at the supermarkets.

"Come on, cousin, I'm sure you'll like it."

We got into her small versatile urban car and headed to a crowded area, bustling with people, full of shops, music, and illuminated advertising signs that promoted everything from needles, shoes, and makeup to a luxury car, diamond rings, or a Rolex. Susan took at least half an hour just to find available parking, and I wondered how long the larger cars would take! We walked along the sidewalk, and everything felt chaotic to me. I felt confused, and it seemed like everyone was staring at me like a strange creature. Perhaps my unbranded and dull clothes were the new fashion trend that caught their attention. We went from store to store, and she had a wide grin on her face, without any remorse, as she pulled out her plastic card that said "American Express" and paid for everything I tried on and liked, from a denim jacket to Nike sneakers. I already had my arms and hands full of shopping bags, and she was still unsatisfied with everything she had bought for me. We got back into the car, and after driving through the traffic in circles, we arrived at a large building called Sears. My jaw dropped when I entered and realized that inside this massive concrete box, you could find everything in one place, from a pair of sockets to a lawnmower, jewelry, televisions, coats, tableware, sports and camping equipment, even aluminum canoes and life insurance in case you drown after falling out of one of them. The escalators were a delight because not only could I rest after walking so much, but I also felt effortlessly elevated to another floor full of curiosities. Susan finally took pity on me and asked if I wanted to go back home, to which I enthusiastically responded, "Yes."

My previous life was very simple. I lived with very little and learned to appreciate other things that brought happiness and well-being to my life. The sea was a special place, my animals were special, and the people who smiled at me and extended a hand, the trees that provided me with food, and the few friends like Alexandra and her mother were what I valued the most. Feeling comfortable meant being able to run without constraints, feeling the sand and the wind, not wearing tight jeans that limited my speed and needing to be cautious to avoid staining the new sneakers. But I had to adapt to this new society that forced me to follow its trends and social standardization, or else I would always be the African oddball.

That night at dinner, sitting at a table overflowing with food on a floral tablecloth and fine dinnerware with golden edges, I looked around at all these new people, smiling faces I had never seen before, all confident in their pursuit of life, blissful in their achievements and possessions, oblivious above all to need, pain, and fear. None of them, except for my father who was sitting in the other corner conversing with his sister, could ever imagine where I really came from and the horrible experiences I had lived through, always on the edge of death. I looked around at all these new faces, these people illuminated by an elegant central lamp, and wondered if they were aware of who they were and how fortunate their comfortable lives were, or if they took it all for granted without gratitude. Have they ever experienced hunger? Have any of them been tied up in chains to receive lashings, or suffered sexual attacks and death threats? Do they sleep peacefully without nightmares and insomnia? Can they imagine what it's like to undergo genital mutilation just for being born in a certain place with such a crazy mother?

I felt very loved, but I had to make an effort to disguise my discomfort of being the center of attention, not because I was shy, but because I was only just unraveling my previously solitary life. To counteract the discomfort, I could only manage to smile. I was safe, there was nothing to fear anymore, but for some reason I couldn't explain, dressed in these new trendy clothes and surrounded by love and mutual curiosity, I felt very alone. That night, I gave my father a tight hug and said thank you in his language, to which he lovingly responded, "You're welcome, sweety."

The exhaustion from everything I had experienced in the past three days couldn't prevent my nightmares from robbing me of sleep that night and granting my heart a little peace.

The next morning, everyone came to the door to say goodbye, and I, very excited, thanked each and every one of them for welcoming me with so much affection and hospitality. We promised to see each other again and said our goodbyes. The plane took off towards California, my new home even further away from my beloved African land.

The sunset bathed the suspension bridge that crossed the entrance to the sea towards the San Francisco Bay with its last rays of sun. My father pointed to it with his finger pressed against the window, explaining to me that it was called the Golden Gate because, with its ochre color, sailors saw it as golden during sunsets when looking at it from the Pacific. As the aluminum bird adjusted its flaps with its giant wings to turn towards the bay and align with the runway, I delighted in looking at the buildings and hills filled with houses, which unlocked the treasure chest of my memories, recalling some photographs my mother had of a city called Valparaíso in her native Chile. They looked very similar, and I mentioned it to my father, who agreed and told me that when he was young, before meeting my mother, he had worked in that southern city. He also told me that across the Golden Gate towards the north, there is a small town full of sailboats called Sausalito and that it has a central plaza called "Plaza Viña del Mar", as a tribute to the sister city called Sausalito in Viña del Mar, which is located next to Valparaíso, that place I only knew through photographs. I began to think that my mother's shadows would follow me wherever I went, bringing the memories of Chile to me in every corner, even behind the airplane window.

"There you can see Alcatraz Island, Andrea. It used to be a high-security prison that ceased to exist when three prisoners escaped and were never found. Al Capone, a famous mobster from Brooklyn, was also imprisoned there," my father said. After a brief silence, I asked him:

"And if my mom comes here, could they lock her up there?" Sam laughed a lot at my comment.

"Yes, my love, of course! We'll lock her up there!"

My father rented a car, and we headed south on Highway 101 toward Hollister. Suddenly, the city lights disappeared, and we were surrounded only by the darkness of those vast agricultural plantations. When we arrived, Monika and Melanie came out to greet us. Katie was already asleep. I immediately thanked Monika for her patience, trying to explain to me that my father had arrived at the Hotel Nina, and she said, "No problem," without giving it much importance. She had no idea that her words, although I understood them little, were crucial in reuniting me with my father and finding the keys to my freedom away from Mrs. Castillo. Monika greeted my father with little enthusiasm, very different from the reception we had in Connecticut. Melanie just looked at me through her oversized glasses and smiled without saying a word, only indicating my room, which was an improvised sofa bed in my father's office. Monika had prepared a light dinner, which we enjoyed before going to sleep.

The next morning, the phone rang while Sam was preparing breakfast for everyone. After greeting the person on the other end, he remained silent, listening attentively for a few minutes. With a dry and tight throat, he could barely say goodbye to the person on the call. He hung up the phone, walked disoriented to the kitchen to pour coffee, and couldn't hold back his tears any longer. Monika arrived immediately and embraced him as he cried like a lost child. I stood at the kitchen door, thinking the worst: they called from the embassy, and they're going to send me back to Africa.

I thought that if that were the case, before he tries to put me in his car to take me to the airport, I would have run through the fields of Hollister and crossed all of San Juan Bautista and beyond until I couldn't be found anymore. But suddenly, Sam composed himself. He washed his face in the sink, wet his hair a little, and took a deep breath. He looked at me and opened his arms for me to walk into his embrace, which I did without hesitation, running to him.

"They just called me to tell me that my father has passed away. I'm so sorry, your grandfather is gone, Andrea. I think he was happy to have met you," he said, placing his hands on my shoulders.

"I have to leave right now and go back to New York," he said, looking at the clock on the wall and comparing the time with his Citizen watch, just as he did when we left the elevator at the hotel. His appetite vanished, and he only drank his coffee. My heart broke seeing him so fragile, showing his most human side. I felt powerless, unable to do anything for this man who had given everything for me, risking his life in a mission almost like a military commando. And now, grief had taken hold of him, pulling him back to New York to mourn his father's passing.

Furthermore, the elderly man suffered a sudden cardiac arrest and ceased to exist. I vividly remembered his loving blue eyes and could see his wrinkled, white, cold, and clean hands that held mine for a few hours. I felt incredibly fortunate to have known him, and I regretted not having had the opportunity to share my life with him. Sam packed his suitcase and went to leave it in his car. He then returned and told Monika not to forget to take me to enroll in school that same day because it was urgent for me to learn English and socialize. He also gave her instructions to take me to the doctor. He hugged and kissed me on the forehead, bid farewell to his wife and daughters, and set off to say goodbye to his father.

From that day on, my new life began in a land as distant as it was different from where I grew up. I was unable to locate the cardinal points in this valley surrounded by hills, and the fear of getting lost without knowing how to return home was always present. Although I had managed to escape my mother's madness, even though I felt safe in this house, I didn't feel welcomed. For some reason, Monika looked at me with a certain disdain, and now that my grandfather had passed away the day after I met him, I felt an aggressive communication barrier beyond language with her. I believe that her imagination suddenly took a superstitious turn, and she started seeing me as a bird of ill omen, carrying with me the negative energies not only from my experiences and my tormentor but also from the devotions and rituals of black and ancestral Africa. She thought that I was the dark shadow that took the soul of the poor old man. I didn't quite understand why she harbored such animosity towards me, but what I began to perceive as the days went by, something I was unaware of, was that her relationship with my father was as worn out as the one he had with my mother.

When Samuel returned from his father's funeral, he was very happy to see me, and his favorite moments were seeing the three daughters gathered and sharing harmoniously. My father was always a man who knew how to listen, and before making decisions, he exhausted resources to measure the consequences, thanks to the patience and extended will that characterized him, even though the likelihood of changing his mind was very remote, as he was stubborn and obstinate by nature. In the case of his relationship with Eugenia, it was an elastic band that stretched and stretched to such an extent that broke irreversibly without ever crossing my father's mind that I would bear the most atrocious consequences. Now, indirectly from my point of view, but directly from Monika's perspective, I felt like I was largely the reason for their disagreements. Their arguments heated up just like this valley does during the summer, surrounded by dry grass, on the verge of scorching and catching. Seeing them both live under the same roof, unable to tolerate each other's presence, immediately took me back to my childhood. Instead of hearing Monika's shouts, I could hear my mother insulting and threatening my father.

Some people validate their unhappiness and the wasted time of their lives in the name of sacrifice for something or someone. Some people spend their entire lives living together but in separate rooms, while others even share the same room but with two distant beds. They allow possessions, children, pets, family, societal expectations, and the avoidance of separating assets and bank accounts to be stronger than their personal happiness and the irreversible seconds of their bitter existence. My father had already reached those limits before, and this time he was unwilling to abandon his self-sacrifice for his little Katie, especially after what happened to me. She was his anchor to this already fragmented home consumed by chronic discord. And now that the family had grown in size with my arrival, he assumed the sacrifice even more fervently, like Christ accepting his crown of thorns, spending the rest of his days enduring the humiliations and resentments of his German wife.

While I was adapting to my new school, to new faces, and unconsciously learning the language rapidly, getting acquainted with different flavors, from fast-food restaurants to the abundance of Mexican cuisine. This was due to the high rate of immigration from the neighboring country that came to work the fields. Back in Senegal, I'm sure my mother was still searching for me in every corner. Her curses and rituals were incapable of dragging me back to her castle of spells, tortures, and orgies.

My father always did his best to anticipate events by strategically planning his steps in life, although life didn't always comply with his desires. One of his concerns was to receive a possible and unexpected visit from my mother in her desperate efforts to capture me and take me back to Africa. To prevent it and be prepared, after a couple of months, Samuel wrote a letter to Ann Sides, the official from the American embassy, who did everything possible to facilitate my departure from the African country.

The note read as follows:

June 9, 1989, Dear Ann Sides,

Many months have passed since we met last September in Dakar, and you were extremely valuable in arranging the necessary details and passport for my daughter Andrea and our departure to the USA under quite unusual circumstances. We both would like to thank you again for your compassion and efforts that went beyond the call of duty. Please accept my apologies for this belated note of appreciation, and please believe that it is no less sincere for arriving later.

Shortly after my return with Andrea and after a brief visit to see him, my father passed away at the age of eighty-eight. It was very special that he had the opportunity to meet his granddaughter for the first time, and you helped fulfill his wishes before his passing, which meant a lot to him and Andrea.

My family here has received her very well, and we have immediately enrolled her in high school where she is quickly learning English and doing well in other subjects. Despite the terrible experiences she has had at the hands of her mother, which have caused her nightmares, she exhibits a fairly normal and balanced behavior in most aspects.

She has shared more atrocities with me, which I won't mention on this occasion, and because of that, she is seeing a psychologist concurrently with the language problem. She is also being evaluated and medically examined to assess her injuries. I have spoken on the phone with her maternal grandmother in Chile, and she has warned me that María Eugenia has made her aware of her plan to come to America and abduct her, taking her first to Mexico and then to Senegal. Given that she has made this threat and has been accused her daughter of child abuse,

I wonder if this would be sufficient to deny her a visa to the United States if she were to apply for one. She has threatened Andrea's life on numerous occasions, even with a gun that was confiscated from her after she was arrested for the kidnapping of a diplomat from Mauritania, who happened to be one of her lovers, a matter that you will recall you have already investigated.

Please also note that she often uses my last name as it suits her, in case she attempts to enter the country under the name Armstrong. Furthermore, I inform you that I met her around 1967, and it was not until recently that I learned she had previously been married to a voluntary military officer from the Peace Corps sent to Chile named Alexander Zipperer, in case she also tries to use another surname as an identity.

My greatest concern right now is keeping my daughter safe and helping her adjust to her new family, and I implore you to do everything in your power to ensure Andrea's well-being is always protected away from this woman.

I await your response and once again, I infinitely appreciate all your help and professional support in this case, where the greatest beneficiary is my daughter, Andrea, who will be able to find a much better life than she had before.

Yours sincerely,

Samuel Armstrong.

Hollister, California.

With her obsession for efficiency, Ann Sides wasted no time in responding to Samuel, stating that she would do everything possible to keep Andrea safe in the USA and escalate the case to the appropriate government agencies. She also mentioned that María Eugenia had turned to Senegal and used all her connections to try to locate the whereabouts of the girl until an unknown person informed her that her daughter had left the country, but not before publishing a notice of her disappearance along with a recent photo of Andrea in the official newspaper.

In Ann's letter addressed to California, she included a newspaper clipping with a photo of Andrea half-smiling, which read:

"June 22, 1986. This girl named Andrea Armstrong ran away yesterday morning, and since then her parents have not heard from her. At the time of her escape from Saldia School in Dieuppeul, she was wearing a blue suit. If seen, please notify the Dieuppeul police station, the director of Saldia School, or contact Armstrong at number 8248 Sicap Sacre Cosur tel 217382."

Upon receiving the correspondence, Samuel fell into deep thought when he noticed that Eugenia had used the word "escape" in newspaper instead of "disappeared" from the school. Did she suspect Andrea's plans to escape? Was her network of contacts so efficient that a disappearance would have been impossible? Then, running his hand through his beard, he realized that what he had told Officer Sides had a solid basis, and here was the proof: María Eugenia never mentioned her name, only the surname Armstrong, and referred to "her parents". Did she feel embarrassed to expose herself to society as a single mother concerned about her daughter's disappearance? Or was her conscience preventing her from accepting that this was bound to happen sooner or later?

Hell Angels

Monika was studying to become a gynecologist. She was a capable and intelligent woman. She possessed qualities very similar to those of my mother, the most prominent being the dual personality she could switch in an instant, just like María Eugenia's two-headed dragon. In her clinic, she could be the sweetest and most fragrant rose, but as soon as she arrived home, she would shed her petals and dress herself in sharp and pointed thorns. My biggest limitation continued to be the ongoing language barrier and for Monika, that was reprehensible for a white girl like me, to the point where she believed I was a fool because I didn't understand anything when, after a couple of weeks in my new home, she started giving me orders and imposing household chores. With her gestures and her loud, aggressive voice, she would show me one by one the things I had to do when I came back from school—chores that I was already very familiar with: cleaning the kitchen, washing the dishes, making the beds, cleaning the bathroom, taking out the trash. I felt bewildered, and since I couldn't ask in English if she was asking me for a favor or forcing me to do all those things, I preferred to say "yes" to everything. That's how she established her dominance over my will, just like Columbus when he buried his sword in his first beach, declaring them the property of the Spanish crown. After a short time, seeing that the new Cinderella of the house was efficient, obedient, and had professional experience, she placed little Katie in my arms, and from then on, I became responsible for changing her diapers and keeping her entertained so she wouldn't cry. I didn't mind that task at all; in fact, it made me feel happy to have a younger sister, and I treated her with great affection.

As for Melanie, she was a different story. She was 14 years old when I arrived and disrupted her peaceful nest. Just like the first day I met her, Melanie hardly spoke to me. Her father was a black man of German nationality who quickly did what was necessary to continue his path and life away from Monika. As a result of their racial mix, she had that tangled afro hair, but with a reddish hue, and her cinnamon skin with blue eyes appeared larger than life behind those huge glasses, which covered her cheeks more than her eyes. She was very thin, and her teeth resembled those of a mule. My father adopted her without any prejudice when he fell in love with that woman who saved him from being imprisoned by the German authorities for playing the role of a trafficker, but for some reason, Melanie didn't have that honest and deep attachment to her adoptive father, despite having known him since she was very young. Melanie took pleasure in letting me know that my presence in her house caused her great indifference, a matter that triggered the opposite effect, as she would go to great lengths to assert her territory. "This is mine, as is that, and that over there is also mine," she would proclaim, thus expressing her deep concern about my unintentional intrusion. It was almost inevitable for her to retain the muscles of her face, which would turn into a mocking smile whenever Monika assigned me household chores. This was particularly irksome because Melanie had no responsibilities herself, fueling her arrogance and clearly establishing her status and hierarchy within the family.

Every morning, my father would take us to school in his truck. As soon as we got out, she would run to her friends, and they would look at me from a distance, exchanging secrets and news about the newly arrived African girl. Her greatest pleasures were harassment and intimidation. She would call me to join her group of friends, and then they would start asking me questions about Africa, lions, arrows, and elephants. I never had a mirror in front of me to see how red I turned from embarrassment when I opened my mouth and responded in my broken English with an African Tarzan accent, struggling to find the words, pronouncing them with a twisted tongue and not opening my lips as widely as those from rural areas do. Then the laughter and imitations of my primitive way of speaking would come, and I didn't know what they were saying about me, I didn't understand it, but jokes of all kinds would spontaneously arise, causing a commotion that drew the attention of the entire school. It squeezed my heart, and though I pretended to find it funny too, I would escape to a corner of the playground or the classroom, holding back my tears. I couldn't understand how I could be surrounded by so many children and still feel so alone. In those moments, despite being in love with the freedom I enjoyed on this continent, I would console myself by imagining being with Ruby, Leopold, Baba, and all my beloved animals with whom we could understand each other perfectly without knowing or sharing any language.

One day, just before vacation, the gang approached with the clear intention of mocking me. Melanie led her club, and they surrounded me in a circle, asking absurd questions and pressuring me to speak. When I answered the first few words, their laughter was like knives in my ears, their eyes burned me, and all those hands pointing at me and pulling my braids felt like demonic snakes ready to devour me. In my desperation, I pushed some of them away and ran frantically to the school's main entrance. From there, I sprinted as if I were running on the beaches and dirt streets of Dakar. I ran without stopping, turning corners until I got completely lost.

When I realized that I was far away from Melanie's harassment and her cruel snakes, I also realized that I didn't know how to get back to school, let alone my home. I sat next to an adobe wall, where large arms of prickly pears peeked out, laden with red fruit, providing shade for my rest. Suddenly, I heard a distant rumble of engines, with deep and low sounds that grew louder by the second, shaking the windows of the house in front of me. After a few minutes, the thunderous noise felt very close. I turned my head to the right and saw that, hundreds of motorcycles began to cross a block away, parading in a caravan, their chrome chassis shining like diamonds in the afternoon sun, proudly roaring their infernal sounds. I stood up from the ground and walked to the next street to satisfy my curiosity and momentarily forget my misery of being lost. Countless bikers passed by, and I could see that they were slowing down further towards the city center, occupying the entire avenue as they pleased. I walked towards this spectacle that I had never seen before and was intrigued to see these people dressed in black leather, both men and women, wearing jackets, gloves with steel-tipped fingers, boots, neck, and mouth bandanas, some with large mustaches, and others with bushy beards. I was impressed by the sight of so many motorcycles in various colors, shiny helmets atop their riders' heads. Some wore skull masks that covered their faces, each one expressing their own unique identity through their clothing and motorcycle. What caught my attention the most was why almost everyone enjoyed riding slowly, even when stationary on their machines, but would accelerate by twisting their wrists on the handlebars to make their exhausts rumble and emit both a deafening noise and bursts of combustion smoke. I felt very alien among all these people with their American flags, eagles, symbolism, jackets with strange logos on their backs like "Hell Angels", "Vagos", "Mongols", an army on their Harley Davidsons, Indians, Triumphs, which were the most prevalent motorcycle brands. Who were these outlaws, and why were they doing this? In Senegal, motorcycles were generally bicycles to which a small two-stroke engine was added, and people bought fuel in recycled soda bottles, which they cherished and avoided wasting a drop. Jackets, pants, leather boots, or helmets were unheard of there. People walked barefoot, and if they wanted a little security and luxury, they wore sandals.

I moved away from the spectacle and came across a small truck that played a monotonous children's song repeatedly through a giant speaker attached to the vehicle's roof. I stopped for a moment to admire the astonishing number of ice cream signs that adorned the truck's exterior. I had never seen anything like it before. In Dakar, a man would walk by singing with a tiny cart that carried two or three things: frozen juice in plastic bags, or if you had more money, you could get a cup of mango or banana milk ice cream. But what was in front of me was a paradise of popsicles and cones on four wheels! As I looked at the colorful signs, a man of Asian appearance, with graying hair but without wrinkles on his face, said something to me from inside the truck. I didn't understand a word because his English, although much more advanced than mine, sounded confusing and strange to my ears. As soon as I turned to continue on my way, he stuck his head out of the window and said, "Wait, wait!" Then, as if by magic, he extended his arm outside, holding a colorful ice cream cone, and with a wide smile on his face. His small, yellow teeth indicated that I should take it.

"No money, no money, sorry!" I said, concerned, to which the man replied, "No money, no money!" and continued smiling. So, I took the ice cream and thanked him as best as I could for his gesture and kindness. As I enjoyed the delicious cone, I felt proud to have finally engaged in my first conversation in English without anyone mocking me; on the contrary, I had been rewarded.

After walking along a long avenue, my concern about not finding the way back began to grow, accompanied by the fatigue in my legs. I sat on a street corner under the shade of a large tree. There, I counted ants, little birds, minutes, leaves, and also my tears. With my head down, I suddenly saw two large wheels come to a screeching halt in front of me. I looked up and immediately recognized that truck. Here was my hero coming to rescue me once again. My father jumped out of the vehicle and ran towards me. He was very angry and scolded me sternly, but then he gave me a tight hug and opened the door for me to get in. He started driving around the city, pointing out where the hospital, the town hall, and the main streets were—an intensive tour that at least made me feel more oriented for the next time I had to escape from Melanie and her cronies. My father explained to me that this week they would be celebrating the independence of the United States, and all those bikers were gathering to celebrate, drink, and make noise at an event called the "Freedom Rally". He also told me that recently the city of Hollister had gained some fame because scenes from the movie *La Bamba* had been filmed there, and people associated Marlon Brando with his character Johnny Strabler, the leader of a violent motorcycle gang called the "Black Rebels" in the movie *The Wild One* from 1950.

Everything started to make sense to me—the embroidered jackets, beards, boots, and helmets—and I began to understand that celebrations in California are grand and loud, much louder than the stretched leather drums in Senegal.

Pennysaver

I witnessed my father's unhappiness every day. When we all sat down for dinner, it was Monika and Sam's favorite moment to start a minor argument that would gradually escalate into shouting at each other without even listening to what they were saying. The baby would start crying, and I would pick her up and take her out of the room. These events happened very often. One morning, Monika stopped me and told me that I needed to find a job to contribute to the household expenses because I couldn't live for free under the same roof anymore. So, I got a job at a small fast-food restaurant called A&W Burgers. In less than a month, I was fired for preparing burgers with onions when they were supposed to be without onions, and for not putting cheese when the order was with cheese, among other mistakes that I barely remember. The manager was a full-fledged racist and only hired me because I was white with colored eyes, just like everyone else who worked there for a measly $4 an hour. Similarly, the clientele was selectively white. I left there and ended up in another restaurant called Taco Bell. I felt much more comfortable there. Almost everyone who worked there was Mexican or Latin American, and if we needed to speak English, we understood each other clearly through hand gestures, eye contact, and whatever else was necessary, but communication flowed. Besides, it had been a long time since I heard the Spanish my mother spoke when she insulted me or when she talked to my grandparents Sergio and Teresa. So Spanish, or "Español" as they call it here, was very easy for me to learn. And to reinforce the language of "the race," I enrolled in school classes, which helped me navigate this part of California where there are significant Spanish-speaking populations. Mexicans and Latinos have a very different sense of humor, and when you add their desire to improve and pursue the American dream, it results in very cheerful, hardworking, and honest people who want to succeed.

Before long, I was able to earn enough income to appease Monika's demands, and the party could continue peacefully for a few days. After almost two years, I had mastered the rebellious language. I was doing well in school, and my father talked to me about pursuing a path towards university. Melanie didn't mock me as much now that I could understand what she said behind my back, but she continued to be aloof and hostile towards me. I sensed something very strange about her, and I had a feeling that I would discover it soon enough. She became an aggressive and unstable little girl. Sam and Monika avoided getting into confrontations with her because she would insult them with a mouth bigger than a whale's and more aggressive than a shark's. If Sam or Monika dared to punish her or confront her, she would open the curtains and the theater would begin, ranging from terrifying screams to calling the police and accusing her parents of being torturers. If only she knew that the only tortured one in this house and this city was me!

I returned from work one afternoon and entered my small room to rest. I left my things on the nightstand and went to the bathroom. In less than two minutes, I returned to my room to find Melanie red-handed, going through my bag. She had patiently waited for the opportunity to steal from me, and there it was, my bag on the bed, and me in the bathroom. The perfect crime, according to her. After giving me a menacing look, she ran out, pushing me without saying a word, and locked herself in her room. I contemplated exposing her, as it would further turn everyone against me, but at the same time, I had to make her realize that she couldn't play games with me anymore. I spoke up and recounted everything in detail when we gathered for dinner. Melanie widened her eyes as if witnessing a miracle or strange phenomenon. She turned red and became hysterical, trying to convince Sam and Monika that what I had just accused her of was a lie. Monika looked at me indignantly, making me feel like I was directly attacking her daughter's morality and integrity, while my father bowed his head without saying anything. I don't know if they took Melanie's demands seriously and no one believed me, or as the Mexicans at my workplace say "les valió madres," - they simply didn't give a damn. In that moment, I felt like the only one who didn't belong in that madhouse. Melanie shouted a few insults at me, got up from the table, and went to her room. Immediately, I did the same, but without saying a single word. It didn't take ten seconds for the shouting match between Sam and his wife to begin. Katie cried, trying to steal the spotlight of the night. They all made me feel like the true villain of the movie: the outsider, the last in line, the African, who unintentionally ruined their dinner and their daughter's reputation. I never thought I would feel the same loneliness that haunted me in Dakar, with the notable difference that there I could alleviate that loneliness with my animals. I had no other reference to compare it to. But, surrounded by these people, my father, and ample freedom, I felt like I had no other choice or another country to escape to. I briefly considered going to Chile, but then the memories of my grandfather, Sergio, unleashed on my mother came to mind, and I immediately dismissed the idea. I would never risk experiencing that fate.

Time passed inexorably. I started working at a Chevron gas station where I learned many things related to the industry: administration, payments, suppliers, regulations, mechanics, oil changes, and so on. I had enough responsibilities for my salary to be somewhat decent this time. Thanks to the many overtime hours, I was able to save significantly, which also helped me avoid a large portion of the obligations imposed on me by Monika at home. She always came home claiming to be tired and sprawled on the couch to watch television. Sometimes I arrived home late after long shifts, but I didn't have those privileges, and my exhaustion never mattered to anyone.

By then, it became increasingly difficult to focus on my studies in high school, not because of a lack of time or even fatigue, but rather due to the toxic treatment and atmosphere that suffocated me upon returning home. This burden weighed on me more each day. This time, I didn't suffer physical punishment, torture, or assaults on my dignity, but I endured a lack of love, indifference, mental abuse, and a persistent tyranny over my infinite will. After nearly four years living under that roof, my patience was a stretched elastic on the verge of snapping, and my heart became a place that housed impotence, shame, and deprivation. My soul ached witnessing my father endure the relentless burdens of his relationship with his wife, like a donkey climbing uphill. In his eyes, I could discern despair, anguish, the urge to explode, to burst like the ion engine of a spaceship and burn everything around him in pursuit of freedom, silence, and the tranquility of infinite space. My Superman was defeated, beaten, and sad. He was unable to distance himself from the Kryptonite particles emitted by Monika. She was that force that trapped everything, like an interstellar black hole, a wormhole, who believed herself to be the executioner of the life of the universes around her, capable of pulverizing us with just a glance.

One certain afternoon, my father was watering the lawn; there was no one else at home. I parked proudly in front of the garden with my first Ford Mustang and my driver's license in hand, a result of the many hours of Sam's hysteria teaching me how to shift gears and step on the clutch, unsuspecting that my first car would ironically be automatic! I got out of the car, and as we looked at each other, we smiled. I approached his side, he hugged my shoulder with one hand, while the other continued watering the plants.

"I can't take it anymore, daughter. This situation is unbearable. I need to divorce this woman as soon as possible. I can't bear any more humiliation!"

He sighed. Then he kept silent for a few seconds and continued:

"I have been thinking about it a lot, and it's something I should have done a long time ago. Would you like us to live together, you and me? Do you like the idea?"

"Of course, Dad, we can split the expenses fifty-fifty!"

Finally, this man had made that decision, which was much easier than going to rescue me in Senegal. My hope resurfaced like a Norwegian spring. After a few days and with a determination stronger than Marco Polo's, we went to a woman who lived with her son in a two-story house in Watsonville, a beautiful place steps away from the sea and the beach, who was willing to rent us the entire second floor. But the weeks passed and passed, and I didn't see any action in this unfinished movie.

Impatient to see that Samuel Armstrong was not taking the initiative, I asked him directly, "When are we leaving?"

"Daughter, I can't. I can't leave Katie. I already made the mistake of running away when you were a baby, and look at the tragic consequences it brought on you. I can't allow your sister to become a victim of this woman. Forgive me for getting your hopes up, and please understand me..."

"I understand, Dad. Don't worry".

I suppressed all attempts to throw the tantrum of the year, and once again, disappointment was the only nourishment for my soul. As a result, on that very day, I resolved to fly for the first time with my own wings. The time had come. The story of my life was maturing enough to be able to annihilate the fear of loneliness once and for all.

PennySaver, a free magazine of classified ads that arrived in the mail was where" I began to search for what would be my first independent home. At least I had already saved up for a decent deposit and a few months' rent. I found a small studio in San Juan Bautista for $400 per month. It consisted of one room, a kitchen, and a bathroom, which was all I needed to start my independent life. My father submerged himself in a lake of mixed emotions—shame, joy, sadness—when he heard me say that the time had come for us to separate. He had no choice but to accept it, and with all his willingness, he helped me move my few belongings into my new home. While both of us were consumed by the melancholy of parting ways, Monika celebrated my farewell. My first months of 1992, alone in that little house almost in the middle of nowhere, were saturated with nostalgia and adorned with the occasional nightmare where my mother tirelessly searched for me with a gun in one hand and her sadistic whip in the other, roaming the streets of Dakar. And when the silence of the night was interrupted by some noise, it felt almost natural to imagine that at any moment, the Doña would open the door to eliminate me once and for all. But I had no choice but to confront all my fears and overcome the burden of feeling abandoned and unprotected. Until I finally accepted that continuous void, which ultimately was much better than enduring another second in that home that accompanied my early adolescence in this country. I had to train my mind to accept these emotional delusions, and in the effort and hustle of tolerating experiences like this, without realizing it, I grew stronger and stronger. This starting from scratch was no longer the unknown dimension, but rather a true opportunity to be free again, like the animals of the savannas of my beloved Africa. About six years went by during which communication with Sam became very distant. His visits to my home were sporadic, although we talked on the phone once or twice a month. In my struggle to survive, I didn't pursue my studies and instead began to get to know myself, taking the time to objectively explore my life's purpose. It was a slow and sometimes distressing process when I felt incapable of overcoming my psychological traumas.

San Benito County became a place where the roads were my daily bread. Sitting behind the wheel with my youth and a desire to discover everything, sometimes I didn't even realize the speed beneath the wheels. I would immerse myself in the image of the road ahead, and the almond, orange, and walnut trees formed a blurry, fast wall on either side, a hazy tunnel guiding me to a destination-less place. At the same time, the horizon transformed into a movie screen where I could relive the most anguishing details of my life. In my wild Mustang, I felt like I could escape with or against the wind, limitless, without distances, without a final direction, transporting myself like light in an infinite escape, without any reason other than the pleasure of fleeing through space and time.

I made some friendships, and I have very little memory of any suitor who tried to steal a kiss from me. While I was attractive to many, I saw only the reflection of a being without self-esteem in the mirror. And that greatly hindered me in any potential relationship. I always felt inferior, of low caliber, of little value. I don't know if any guy could ever perceive my lack of ego, pride, and confidence, but in any case, nothing worked out. During that time of my youth, I couldn't help but feel and think that guys only wanted a moment of hormonal excitement, without taking responsibility for my loneliness. Once again, an animal, a beautiful cat, came into my life and brought not only companionship and good intentions but also a complete disinterest in taking advantage of me in any way. We were now three: the cat, the loneliness, and me, and without any effort, we started getting along better than ever before

Downhill

My father had many acquaintances but few friends. One of his friends was our neighbor, Wade, who had an accident when he was hit by a vehicle while cycling in the vicinity of the neighborhood. Wade lived alone and began his recovery with the help of Monika, who would visit his house two or three times a day to bring him food and assist him in any way she could. The astute reader will notice that Monika, like my mother, also carried a kind and compassionate burden that she would unleash as she saw fit.

After a couple of months had passed, Wade was able to walk with the support of a crutch, and one Friday morning, he went out to soak up the sun just as Samuel was loading things into his truck to go camping with his daughter, Katie.

"Are you going camping, Sam?"

"Hello, Wade! Yes, you know me. Do you want to come with us? I have extra food, beers, and another tent. It'll do you good!"

"Thank you for the invitation, my friend, but I'm not feeling very well this morning. Maybe next time. Enjoy yourselves!"

Samuel and Katie set off happily on their camping trip towards Mount Madonna, a place not too far away, nestled in a coastal mountain range filled with lush vegetation, wildlife, and adorned with towering sequoias. On Saturday afternoon, the weather suddenly changed and rain poured down, drenching everything. Sam decided to return home a day earlier than planned. Upon arriving home, he parked the truck temporarily to move Monika's car, which was occupying the covered porch.

"Don't get out yet, Katie. I'll get the keys and move the car. Wait for me here."

Sam entered through the side door and, as he reached for the keys hanging next to the door, an irresistible urge to urinate overcame him. He walked down the hallway towards the bathroom and heard some noises that made him forget about the pressure in his bladder. He peeked into his room and opened the door. He opened the door shouting, "Monika! Monika!"

There she was, his wife, naked, giving an intensive therapeutic session to their neighbor and friend Wade, in an effort to help him recover from his accident once and for all. Sam entered a state of hysterical shock, turning red and sweaty. He lunged at his newly minted "ex-friend" with all his masculine brutality, kicking him out of the house. Amidst the punches, scratches, and Monika's screams, the injured man tried to dress himself, completely forgetting his injuries. The commotion was so intense that it alarmed not only Katie, who was still waiting in the truck, but also the neighboring residents, who undoubtedly were the ones to call the police. Desperate, Monika yelled insults at Sam, telling him that violence was not the way to confront things and that he should take his rage back to the mountains where it came from. Samuel, uncontrollable, grabbed her by the throat and almost strangled her, but at the same time, he exploded and couldn't take it anymore. His body, mind, stress, and disillusionment cornered him to the point where his heart gave out.

When I received the call from the hospital, I made my way down the road, thinking until the last second that none of this was true, that the margin of error was greater than reality. But everything was confirmed when I saw my father asleep, intubated, sedated, and monitored on the hospital bed. From then on, Sam slowly spiraled downhill with each passing year. By the time my father was discharged from the hospital, Monika had already packed her belongings, avoiding another battle and the shame by leaving the house.

She didn't get very far. She immediately settled with Wade, and to this day they remain together, married now. Monika completed her education, financed by Sam, and pursued her career as a gynecologist.

Disillusioned and angry with her mother, Katie decided to stay and live with our father for about four years until she finished college. Later, she moved to Santa Cruz to continue her university studies, and, over time, she was seduced by the gynecologist and her money, which could buy her anything. Meanwhile, Melanie slipped into the abyss of drugs, and I didn't hear from her or her adventures until much later.

Having endured so much throughout my life, I had reached a point where my sole purpose was to find peace. I didn't want money, material possessions, titles, or recognition in social circles. I simply wanted tranquility and to focus on my projects, which were not ambitious but very important. One of them was to defy my destiny and the psychological imposition my mother had chronicled upon me, that I was worthless, that I was nobody. I tried to distance myself as much as possible from anything that caused me emotional turmoil, and that included my father, allowing him to take control of his own life without my intervention. But the man was stubborn, and his soul of a gentleman and adventurous spirit never left him. Soon enough, he met Patricia (ironically sharing the same name as my mother's sister, for those who doubt the power of African magic!), a woman at least 20 years younger than him.

He sold the house and almost all his belongings, purchased a Thousand Trails membership—a company that offers camping resorts across the country—and then invested in a comfortable motorhome, where he could live without many attachments to anyone. Except Patricia. She became his new problem.

With Patricia, they devoted themselves to traveling from California to Washington, from Oregon to Nevada, and beyond. But my father's "sugar daddy" side was more sugar than daddy, and he suffered another heart attack. He was later diagnosed with diabetes and hypertension, and his health problems accumulated one by one, limiting his wanderings, his travels, and above all, his wallet. During that time, he began writing a book about his life story, which he kept on a first-generation laptop. They both returned in October 2005 after a week in Hawaii, and Sam didn't feel well. It didn't take long for Patricia to shamelessly enter his trailer to pick up some things and find him bedridden and without any motivation.

"I'm sorry, Sam. I don't know how to tell you this. I'll be direct: You're old, sick, and poor. There's nothing I can do for you. I wish you the best. Goodbye."

My father couldn't find the words to respond. He tried to get up to chase after Patricia and show her that he was just tired. But he couldn't do anything and sank into his helplessness, welcoming a deep depression that ultimately caused him to have another heart attack. All he managed to do was dial 911 before losing consciousness, and paramedics were dispatched who kept him alive until they loaded him into a helicopter and flew him to the hospital in Salinas. There, after a delicate intervention, they implanted a brand-new pacemaker in his chest. He spent over a month in that hospital, and on the day he was discharged, I went to pick him up so we could have lunch together. He had recovered well, looking strong, robust, and joyful, and we were both happy to share and celebrate a new lease on life once again.

"I'm going to spend Thanksgiving in San Luis Obispo with my cousin. Would you like to come with me?" he said.

"Of course, Dad! I'd love to. I'll drive, we can take my car. How does that sound?" I replied.

I marked this Thanksgiving event with Sam on my calendar, and my workplace was understanding enough to provide me with all the necessary accommodations. As the date of the celebration approached, I called him to finalize the last preparations for our trip.

"Hi, Dad. How are you feeling? I'll come pick you up early the day after tomorrow, okay?" I asked.

"Andrea, it won't be possible. I'm sorry. It's just that Patricia has apologized and been very loving. I'm going to San Luis Obispo with her. Do you understand?" he replied.

"No, Dad, I don't understand. But don't worry, go with her and have a good time," I said.

I hung up the phone and grabbed the sleeve of my blouse to wipe away my tears. I had been looking forward to spending a few days with Sam as a family, thinking it would do us good to get away from everything. I couldn't understand my father's actions, how he could, despite his heart condition and diabetes, be so blind and foolish to believe in that opportunistic woman again. It took me a few days to overcome this new disappointment, and I did so by thinking that if it made him happy, his happiness would help him heal. I stopped dwelling on the matter. Another month passed, and one day, to my surprise, I received a call from his sister, whom I had met many years ago in Connecticut on the day I set foot in the United States. After exchanging greetings, she asked about my father.

"Andrea, I have been trying to reach your father for days, but I haven't been able to locate him. Is he with you? Are you taking care of him?"

"Well, Aunt, I haven't heard from him in weeks. Don't worry, I'll go see him and tell him to call you."

The next day, on December 11th, to my even greater surprise than my aunt's unexpected call, Patricia got on the phone to tell me that Sam had taken a turn for the worst and was once again admitted to Watsonville Hospital. I didn't wait a minute longer and jumped into my car to reach the hospital. As I entered his room, I could only keep silent and swallow hard to hold back the emotion of seeing that man, once as big as a bear, who held me with all his strength at the elevator exit of Hotel Nina, reduced to almost half his size. He had shrunk, become thin and feeble. His beard was too big for him, his eyes had sunk, and his hands were nothing but bones and veins. It was a pitiful sight, to see him so frail, helpless, with dry skin and cracked lips. His skin had clung to his skeleton, his muscle mass had disappeared. I couldn't understand it, and it was hard for me to recognize him. How could this have happened when just a couple of weeks ago, my superhero had risen again like the Phoenix! Patricia arrived silently and peered through the door of the room while I stood beside my father, holding his hand to feel his cold body.

"What happened, Patricia? Why is he like this?"

"These past few weeks, he started feeling very ill. Since we returned from San Luis Obispo, his diarrhea, vomiting, and tachycardia didn't stop."

"But why didn't you let me know? Why didn't you bring him to the hospital earlier? Did you give him his medication when you were with him?"

"You don't understand anything, girl. It's not my fault. I did what I could. They took away his RV, and since then, he has been staying at my place, and I tried to take care of him with what I had. Don't ask me for more."

I remained silent and turned my attention back to my father, the man who had changed my life forever and rescued me from the clutches and madness of María Eugenia, saving me from spending the rest of my days attending to an aboriginal man in a lost tribe in Africa. In front of me was this noble being who always sacrificed something for others without expecting anything in return. He had a urinary infection, a lung infection, intravenous blood clots, and other serious conditions that had led him to a complete collapse. He needed someone to administer his medications, to assist him, and I was absolutely certain, seeing Patricia's indifferent gaze and behavior, that she did the bare minimum not to stop the situation, but to accelerate it and bring it to an end as quickly as possible. And I had to find out the reason, but this wasn't the time to start doing that. The priority was to be there for my father. I didn't know what to do to ease his pain. His legs had turned purple, and there was a risk of amputation.

During the hours of waiting, sitting by his side, anxious for any reaction, it didn't take much for me to unravel the tangled thread and discover that the RV my father had bought, which was his home, had been registered in both his and Patricia's names. Then I remembered that my father had told me some time ago that the vehicle, valued at many thousands of dollars, had a structural flaw, and the insurance company had accepted his claim and would send a hefty check to cover the contract and damages, but not before taking possession of the vehicle. And of course, as soon as Patricia found out about this, she became "loving" with my father again and took him away from spending Thanksgiving together, deceiving him again, the same way you would offer lettuce to a hungry and blind dog. I'm absolutely sure that my father would have given her half of that refund, but that wouldn't be enough for Patricia. She wanted both halves and everything she could get by practically declaring herself the heir to whatever Sam might leave behind. There was no other explanation, and the wicked scheme was evident on its own. The truck to tow that trailer was under my name, but it was also at Patricia's house. However, for me, all these matters became secondary because my priority was Sam's recovery. But it wasn't happening. The doses of morphine were no longer sufficient, and the man would occasionally open his eyes to gaze blankly at the ceiling, unable to recognize me, but squeezing my hand with the last bit of strength he had, futilely trying to escape his pain.

It was almost five o'clock in the morning when I kissed him on the forehead and said goodbye, whispering that I would go home to take a shower and eat something, promising him that I would return in the morning. By the time I got out of the shower, the on-call doctor called me and informed me that Sam had passed away.

I cried as much as I needed to, and then some. I spread the photographs I had collected during our time together on my bed, reliving the few happiest moments of my life as I traveled through my memories to Senegal, repeating his smile over and over again in my mind. I didn't want to remember him the way I saw him in his final moments. On the contrary, I made an effort to forcefully engrave the best moments we shared. My soul ached, and I needed to embrace him one more time.

Later that same day, Patricia called me in an authoritative and rude tone, not caring about my pain in the slightest:

"I need Samuel's wallet and identification. Do you have them?"

"Why are you talking to me like this? Who are you to ask me for my father's things? I am his daughter, I will take care of everything. Show some respect for his death and my grief!"

I couldn't believe it. On that day, I was literally lost in anguish and sadness, and this disrespectful and insensitive woman was talking to me about such things without even expressing her condolences. I immediately thought that my suspicions about the insurance money were true and that this shameless woman took advantage of my father's condition, abandoning him like a leech once she had drained him of all his money and vitality.

No one had visited Samuel during his final days in the hospital, except for this audacious woman and me. My sister Katie showed up that morning after his passing to collect his belongings, including his wallet with his identification, the treasure that Patricia was desperately searching for. She also took the beautiful watch that had traveled the world attached to my father's wrist. Patricia's "gold digger" nature wanted those documents to obtain the correct information and forge Samuel's signature in order to claim the insurance refund. I don't know how she managed it, but she succeeded in her mission, nonetheless. She also kept the truck. And the computer.

None of what little my father had left interested me in the slightest. I didn't want to deal with this woman or any of the procedures that awaited me. My only focus was grieving the loss of my father, the man who had changed my life and rescued me from the clutches and madness of María Eugenia, saving me from spending the rest of my days attending to an indigenous man in a lost tribe in Africa. The noble being who always sacrificed something for others without expecting anything in return was in front of me. He deserved my love, respect, and a proper farewell.

The days went by, and suddenly I remembered the book my father was writing on his laptop. It contained many of the words I share in my own story and other anecdotes of Mr. Armstrong and his exploits. I pleaded with Patricia to return the computer, telling her she could keep whatever she wanted; I only wanted to rescue my father's words that bore witness to my own life. Katie also insisted that she return the laptop, but the wretched woman told her that she had sold it and that we could rot. Only the images of Samuel sitting under that beautiful oak tree, writing, surrounded by the nature he loved, remain in my memory. When he saw me arrive, he would read me a few paragraphs and continued telling me his stories verbally until the sunset. After those occasions, we usually prepared dinner together, and those were some of the best moments of my life.

I tried to recover the truck by going with the police to remove it from Patricia's house without facing her directly. The woman came out of her lair like a madwoman, shouting and insulting me in a rude and uncontrolled manner, even though I was behind the police vehicle. After forcing her to be quiet and talking to her, the sheriff came back and told me that the woman had possibly forged the signature and sold the vehicle. Unfortunately, they couldn't do anything more but escalate the case to a legal trial in court. However, I gave up due to the sheer panic of encountering that woman once more. I never heard from that gold digger thereafter. I sank into a deep depression for months, where the sunlight became unbearable and the nights eternal. Only my cat witnessed the horrors that such great loneliness caused in me.

Many times, I was tempted to try drugs or at least learn how to prepare some African recipes that my mother used to make to calm my anxiety and panic. I would bite my lips and chew my nails (I still do), sitting for hours on end in my armchair, staring into nothingness, scratching my head and running through my thoughts, observing the silence and being stuck in the why of it all.' Why was it so difficult for me to find the happiness, harmony, and peace I never had? What had I done in this bitter life to deserve these punishments over and over again? Wasn't everything my mother did to me enough? Was the bloodied voodoo not sufficient?"

The smoldering curse of Eugenia transcended time and distance, haunting me wherever I went. What more do you want, Mom, for fuck's sake! What more do you want?

Several months passed without any clear direction in my life. Everything became gray and silent. I looked through some photos of my father, and suddenly I saw his Volkswagen bus and thought, *'This man's passion was traveling.' Traveling... of course! That's what I'll do!*

And from every dollar I started earning from that day on, I divided it in two, saving one part to embark on travels just like my father did. That's how I began to emerge from my burrow and escape the clutches of a deep depression and the lingering shadows of the mental burdens passed down to me by María Eugenia."

Bodyguard

A couple of years before my father passed away in 2002, we had just finished having lunch together when, perhaps out of sheer boredom, he said to me:

"Do you want to call your grandfather in Chile? I heard he's very ill."

"Really? I don't know, Dad, I wouldn't know what to say..."

"Just greet him and let them know you're doing well. After all, they're your family, whether you like it or not."

"If you say so..."

"Do it, besides, you already know how to speak Spanish!"

I couldn't hide my nervousness as I watched his fingers dial the numbers and then he handed me the receiver.

"Hello, I would like to speak with Mr. Sergio Castillo."

"Hello? Hello? Who is this?"

"It's me, Andrea, Sergio's granddaughter..."

My memory traveled at the speed of light, exploring every corner of my brain to immediately recognize that deep, hoarse voice that spoke to me... I felt a rush of coldness at the back of my neck, and for some reason, I saw myself as tiny, small, fragile, motionless, capable of doing nothing, invalid and vegetative, unable to even hang up the phone...

"Andrea? Hello, daughter, it's your mother."

There was a deadly silence. A profound, wide pause without haste.

"Hello, Mom..."

"Hello, daughter, how are you? It's been such a long time!"

I looked at my father, and he gestured with his hands and shook his head, silently urging me to keep talking. Then he covered his mouth and looked at me incredulously, remaining completely silent. Fifteen years had passed without knowing anything about each other, and when we started talking, I couldn't believe what was happening. María Eugenia Castillo García Huidobro was speaking directly to me! She told me that she had recently returned to Chile and was leaving Senegal behind, sharing her new plans, her health issues, her travels, and the family. She mentioned that her father had passed away and that she had delivered a farewell speech at the Military Academy, which was a funeral with great honors. She spoke and spoke without stopping, as if there were no more minutes left in life, as if nothing had ever happened, as if we had seen each other yesterday. She sounded kind, laughed, with humor and warmth. It was all very strange, a sensation too difficult to put into words, a moment that could span many pages of this book. Moreover, that was the first time we conversed in Spanish and not in French. She didn't even realize that I had mastered the language!

After the passing of my grandfather Sergio, my mother stayed at his house in Las Condes, an affluent neighborhood in Santiago. She was in the process of receiving her father's inheritance and, on the other hand, solidifying her definitive return to Chile.

In Senegal, my mother managed to buy several properties and acquire an invaluable and extensive collection of African cultural objects. Among her top priorities was bringing a couple of containers filled with authentic items from those lands, as she was organizing the opening of a museum-cultural exhibition. Eugenia kept talking incessantly, and it was very difficult for me to concentrate on her words because my mind was thousands of kilometers away and many years in the past, incessantly bringing bitter moments from my childhood and youth.

"You're going to be a very rich woman, daughter. I'm preparing my will, in which you are the universal heiress of our family's fortune. Let me take a pencil... give me your address so I can write it down."

Without ever thinking about any future consequences, I gave her my address, and since then, we started writing to each other periodically. My mother insisted on letting me know that she was now a very wealthy woman, and had a lot of money and many properties, subtly hinting at her desires for me to return to Chile and live with her. Every time she said the same thing, she would end the conversation by saying that she was sick and tired, that she had cancer and other complications. In her mind, of course, she wanted me back not only to take care of her but perhaps also to become her slave again. She was skilled with words and knew how to manipulate and convince anyone without revealing their true intentions. We talked for over three hours, and when I hung up, my father had fallen asleep in the armchair. María Eugenia never mentioned him, nor did I mention her.

Eugenia didn't know me. She never knew me. She wouldn't understand that her blackmail and offers only disgusted me, and made me feel distrustful of her anew. My heart only wanted to hear an apology, an "I love you," a "forgive me for everything." But none of that came out of her mouth. What was going on in her mind, my God? Did she think I would fly to her side the next day? Did she think all her wealth would be enough to bury the tragedy of my life forever? Did she forget everything she did to me? Doesn't she understand that I feel ashamed to be with a man because she took away my womanhood, my dignity, my purity, my right to feel? It was very difficult to tolerate her strange way of thinking once again, and I think I agreed to stay in contact with her because at least from a distance, she couldn't harm me.

One night, I realized that what I longed for from my mother were things I never had the opportunity to tell her, and perhaps that's why she didn't realize how absurd and incoherent she sounded offering me all the riches of Babylon. So, I took a piece of paper and a pencil and wrote to her in a "nice" manner, letting her know my demands:

"…You have never asked for forgiveness for everything you did to me, you have never told me why you singled me out. All I wanted was for you to be my mother, to love me, to respect me, to treat me as such and not as trash or a slave. You caused me so much pain, and to this day, the scars still haunt me. You also did the same to my father, who at least had the option to escape, but instead, I had to endure your madness and cruelty for years and years…"

That's what the first letter I sent to her address said, to which she never responded. Some time passed, and María Eugenia called me to tell me that she was very ill and wanted to see me, asking me to please come to Chile. She spoke of her dramas with such conviction that I believed her. If seeing me was her last wish, I would grant it. I told my father what was happening, and he couldn't accompany me because he was dealing with his own issues and fearing that Eugenia would drug me, kidnap me, or make me disappear, my father contacted a younger friend of his, of Argentine-Italian descent, and pleaded with him to be my bodyguard on my trip to Chile, with all expenses paid. The man didn't speak much Spanish, but he understood it perfectly, and that was enough to ensure that nothing would happen to me. I thought about it again, took a deep breath, and with my personal security friend, we boarded the plane and flew to South America. By the time we arrived, we agreed to tell everyone that we were just old friends and that he had always wanted to visit Chile, and this was his opportunity. It was the summer of 2004.

The trip was very peaceful, and most of the time, I didn't even dwell on the reality that was about to unfold. In a way, my mind isolated me from any thoughts related to this reunion with my mother. It wasn't until the plane touched Chilean soil that I opened my consciousness and eyes to reality. Before that moment, it had all been a simple tourist trip, but now it was a journey of terror.

When the wheels touched down at Arturo Merino Benitez Airport, I instinctively grabbed my friend's hand and held it tightly. Fear overwhelmed me, and I barely knew if I would be able to get up from my seat and exit the aircraft. I felt that time was moving very slowly backwards, I looked at people, but I didn't see their faces. I was enveloped in a feeling of being completely lost in space, and I regretted in that very moment what I was doing. My friend put his other hand over mine and reassured me, promising that nothing would happen, and that whatever brought me here, he would help me face it. At that moment, I thought that my father's idea of providing me with human protection wasn't so absurd.

After picking up our suitcases, we started walking to the reception area. I am grateful to my suitcase for its great support because without it, I wouldn't have been able to walk due to nerves.

I immediately recognized her. There she was, the gypsy, broader, older, with her black hair tied-up and a silk scarf around her neck. A long black dress revealed chunky and rough-heeled shoes but impeccably shiny. In her hands, she wore several bracelets, and around her neck, a pure gold medallion. Combined with her typical Egyptian-style eye makeup, she exuded a powerful and intriguing image. She had shed her African attire, only wearing one or two native bracelets, but her hands remained a showcase of African craftsmanship. Each finger was adorned with pieces that were impossible to find anywhere in Chile, or even from Ushuaia to Alaska.

She also recognized me from a distance and raised her arm stiffly, moving only her hand, like a true Maneki-neko, the Chinese fortune cat. Her face displayed a slight smile, a mix of yes and no, halfway between ordinary and refined. The strangest thing happened when I was just a step away from her. It wasn't just the heavy and piercing energy that permeated everything within a 20-meter radius; it was that I felt small beside her, despite being almost the same height. For some inexplicable reason, in that moment, I felt that she was much taller and larger than me, more significant than when she would lunge at me or torture me.

My friend stopped, we looked at each other, and I nodded slightly, signaling for him to let me move forward...

"Hello, Mom," I said, almost stammering, with a strange smile and tears welling up in my eyes.

"Welcome to Chile, my daughter. How was your flight?" she said giving me a cold, light embrace. She smelled of clean clothes, cigarettes, and expensive perfume.

"It was fine, Mom. I came with a friend who's always wanted to visit Chile, and I invited him."

"Is he your boyfriend?"

"No, mother, he's just a friend. Let me introduce him. His name is Rob."

"Pleased to meet you, ma'am," Rob said cordially, extending his hand, to which my mother, with her distinguished and exquisite demeanor, also extended hers, this time with a mischievous smile of questionable intent.

I thought that this moment would be worthy of the best Venezuelan telenovela, but instead, it was as if we had seen each other just yesterday. She appeared relaxed, emanating an unwavering aura of iron, without remorse, regrets, or weaknesses exposed. She guided us to her impeccable car and gave us a tour of the city:

"What you see here is called Santa Lucía Hill. Originally, it was called Huelén in the Mapuche language until it was taken by the Spanish conqueror Pedro de Valdivia and his army in 1540, and that's when…" And she continued narrating with details about every important point in the Chilean capital. She was an expert at it, and she did it so well that for a moment I thought it wasn't her, but a professional tour guide we had hired, just like she was in Rio de Janeiro when she captivated the attention of Samuel Armstrong. We finally arrived at my grandfather's house. The place where it all began.

"Come in, daughter, welcome to your home. I hope you like it."

The property resembled a mausoleum, cold as a tomb, filled with luxury and military memorabilia on the walls. She showed us our rooms and took us around every corner. She put on the kettle and prepared tea with butter cookies. As we sat in the living room, she got up to fetch some sugar, and I looked at Rob and told him not to drink the tea. Rob looked at me and whispered, "She didn't add anything suspicious; I saw it when she made it, don't worry."

My mother returned, and we continued conversing and looking at photos of our grandparents until nightfall, when we bid each other goodnight. She slept in my father's bed. On the other side, my room was dark, characterless, with original mid-century style furniture. That night, I remembered all my hardships and locked my room "just in case any unwanted visitors, be they flies or the ghosts of the general, wanted to pay me a visit." Rob was placed on the second floor, which made me uneasy, but I promised myself that if anything happened, I would scream at the top of my lungs to wake him up.

Before going to bed, I went to the kitchen to get a glass of water. Next to the kitchen, there was another door that suddenly swung open as I was filling the glass. I got scared. An elderly, but well-preserved woman appeared and smiled at me, saying:

"I knew that one day I would meet you, my little Andrea. My name is Guillermina, the family's servant. Welcome."

"Hello, pleased to meet you, Mrs. Guillermina. My father told me about you."

"Yes, yes, I remember. A very good man. Well, I'm going to bed. Tomorrow I'll make corn pie for all of you!"

"Thank you very much, Guillermina. I'm looking forward to trying your pie. Good night."

The next day, both Rob and I, along with my mother, enjoyed that typical Chilean dish lovingly prepared by Guillermina. Gradually, this woman with a sincere and kind gaze, but few words, won my affection, and I won hers. She provided me with the tranquility I needed within the house, and every time I saw her, she offered me something from her kitchen full of flavors. In the end, I believe Guillermina's kitchen was the only space where life, colors, and aromas permeated everything, making the rest of the house a habitable place. I looked at this house with Eugenia inside, and I thought that perhaps for me, ostentation, comforts, luxury, fashion, makeup, and social disguise were irrelevant things because I grew up with things of little material importance. If I experienced hunger firsthand, it was due to my mother's deranged decisions, not because of a lack of means to obtain food. In reality, I always had everything, except for what I treasured the most and was always scarce: love.

During the following days, María Eugenia took us all around Santiago, visiting the Castillo and García Huidobro families. Uncles, aunts, nephews, and cousins crossed paths with me, warmly greeting me wherever we went, and offering us something to eat. I was surprised by how fond they were of cigarettes, Coca-Cola, and bread with "chancho" or "palta". In the United States, people have become conscious, and unlike here, they have tried to quit sugary sodas and tobacco. In fact, I was amazed to see people smoking inside their homes, a habit that is not well-regarded in Armstrong's country. Eugenia also invited friends to the house to meet me. Suddenly, I started paying more attention to what Eugenia said about me. She took advantage of those moments when I was distracted or more distant to tell anyone who crossed her path that my father had kidnapped me when I was five years old, with a tone of concern, yet feeling very proud of it.

She claimed that after seventeen years, she had rescued me from the clutches of that man. When she finished her story, she felt deserving of an Oscar and Guinness recognition for the best mother in the world. That angered me greatly.

Rob and I decided to go explore the city, but instead, we took taxis and went to each of those families to set the record straight that the story my mother was spreading was not true. We arrived at Eugenia's sister's house, my aunt Patricia, before she committed suicide, along with her two daughters who had come to visit her from Brazil, and I clarified to all of them that it wasn't true, that my mother, for some of her crazy reasons, was distorting the story. It didn't require a calculator or an abacus to figure out that 17 + 5 equals 22. I was 32. She had erased 10 years of my life!

A few days passed, and my mother rented an apartment facing the beach in Reñaca, a beautiful coastal area very close to Viña del Mar, where bronzed bodies of Argentinians who come to spend their vacations in Chile, as well as the more affluent class from Santiago, often stroll during the summer. Our first stop was a restaurant owned by an old friend of my mother's, and there we tried some typical dishes, among which I enjoyed seafood empanadas accompanied by a chilled white wine. After ordering coffee and dessert, she went to chat with her friend, who barely had time to pay attention because the restaurant was full. I informed Rob that I would go to the bathroom, and as I passed by my mother and her friend talking, I overheard her telling the same story that she had created in her mind. I was her trophy, her banner, her totem, her victory.

We stayed the entire weekend, and by the time Sunday arrived, I only had two more days left before returning to California. That afternoon, my mother sat down to rest on a bench in a park overlooking the sea. Rob kept his distance, and I sat next to her. I looked at her, and she smiled kindly. It was a simple gesture that I couldn't recall receiving throughout all those years. It was a peculiar experience, and in a way, I felt a deep love and compassion for the woman who brought me into this world, even though she had taken from me the very essence of what makes life fulfilling.

We remained silent, watching the children playing in the sand, listening to the waves, the barking of dogs, the vendors offering their wafer cones and "cuchuflís" filled with dulce de leche or ice cream. Seagulls glided above our heads, propelled by a warm, clean, gentle breeze. I never lost hope that this would be the perfect, unrepeatable, and unique moment when María Eugenia would take my hand, look me in the eyes, and ask for forgiveness for everything she had done to me. I was ready to embrace her, desperate to hear, even once, a word of love, a gesture of remorse. But that didn't happen until she said to me, "We're going to be late, it's time to go, daughter."

Without a second thought, I convinced myself that another opportunity like that moment would not repeat itself, and I replied:

"Why did you do all of that to me, Mom?"

She turned her head away from mine and stared at the hazy hills of Valparaíso that touched the distant horizon and the southern clouds. After an eternal silence, she murmured:

"Because you deserved it. That's why."

"I was a child, you abused me, tortured me, sold me, made them mutilate me, you abandoned me. It was because of you that I was raped and almost killed countless times. What did I do to deserve all of that?"

Eugenia stood up and began walking back to the apartment to collect our things. I was glued to my seat, as if I'd been plied with superglue, my tear-filled eyes staring at the horizon. I gathered strength from within and managed to stand up hurriedly to catch up with her and say from behind,

"Why are you telling people that my father kidnapped me, and you rescued me? Why are you saying I'm 22 years old?"

"It makes me look younger. Stop with the nonsense and let's go, we're running late."

I could barely contain my anger, my frustration. Eugenia was an impenetrable wall, not a molecule of remorse existed within her, and my constant fear of waiting for any retaliation from her only made me bite my tongue and not utter another word. I did my best to understand her, but my logic ultimately overcame my feelings, and I told Rob that this woman was more mentally unstable than I thought. We arrived in Santiago that night, and my mother immersed herself in her own thoughts.

She had a bottle of whiskey that lasted until the early hours of the morning only because she mixed it with Coca-Cola; otherwise, it would have lasted only an hour. She woke up on Monday afternoon when Rob and I had our suitcases ready by the door, and I said goodbye to Guillermina, like the grandmother I never had. However, when it came to Eugenia, the parting felt as detached and chilly as bidding farewell to a stranger. I embraced her, and she, with her tousled hair and the scent of alcohol clinging to her, returned the gesture, leaving me uncertain whether it was to steady herself or to bid adieu. Without any noteworthy incidents, we hailed a taxi and made our way back to the United States.

Furious Rage

I returned to California with my heart unsatisfied, with an immense longing for a motherly embrace, with hopes of reuniting with the woman who only existed in my imagination. I felt disappointed and sad, with a tremendous desire to tear certain pages from the story of my life and never remember or mention them again. But it only took' a couple of weeks before my mother started calling me periodically to tell me about the tragedies and hardships of her daily life. Each call was a new drama.

One day, she would tell me that she broke her nose from falling, according to her, because of the medications, and the next day, she would say she bruised her arm or knee, and that everyone was chasing her and wanting her money, and she couldn't trust anyone. She was incapable of recognizing that her dependency on alcohol was rapidly shortening her life. Sometimes I would talk to Guillermina, and she would keep me updated on the tragedy of her boss, how Eugenia's demons wanted to suffocate her because they were tired of her miserable existence and being drunk and drug-dependent all the time. Other times, when she managed to hold off drinking for a few days, she would call me to tell me about her illnesses and how she felt unwell, how one remedy caused this and another caused that. She would tell me that the doctors "looked at her with different eyes" and that she didn't want new romantic or sexual commitments. She would talk about politicians, Chilean corruption, and any drama she could find to make me feel that I should take responsibility and take care of her as soon as possible.

She never forgot to let me know that there was a fortune waiting for me and that I was the universal heir to everything. Her blackmail was clear. Her manipulation reached such outrageous limits that it made me laugh because of how brazen her disguised proposals were.

At that moment, simultaneously, I had to deal with the misfortunes and calamities of my father Samuel and his bloodsucker wife, so there came a point where, for my own mental health and emotional stability, I had to choose to detoxify myself from so much tragedy in order to deal with my own. I started by trying not to answer my mother's calls anymore, or at least spacing out the times I would attend to her. Until one day, after not having spoken to her for at least a month, I picked up the phone with the sole intention of helping her vent once again because I believed even Guillermina wasn't listening to her and was avoiding her by simply locking herself in her room to do her embroidery. In fact, it was then that I began to realize why Guillermina would stick her nose out of her room just enough, like Jerry hiding from Tom, just as I first met her.

I don't know how, but my mother found out that I had gone to tell the truth to the family and debunk her false testimony, according to her, with the purpose of "looking younger". Since then, everyone started distancing themselves from her, and I think each one ended up convincing themselves that she was crazier than they thought, or some screw in her head was literally loose. If anyone had suspicions that Eugenia was strange, well, now they had proof. Her social circle had definitely abandoned her; hardly anyone visited or answered her calls, except for me, who despite everything always gave in. Like that time:

"Hello, Mom?"

"How could you, Andrea! How dare you, you damn bitch!"

"What are you talking about, Mom?" I asked, almost entering a state of nervous shock that prevented me from even moving my arm to hang up, but deep down, immediately understanding the reason for her fury.

"How could you make me look bad in front of the whole family?! How could you come to humiliate me? Now everyone is talking about me, and because of you, my prestige, my reputation, and my name are at stake! I'm going to kill you, you wretch!"

With my chin and the hand holding the receiver trembling uncontrollably, I took a deep breath, gathered my courage, and replied...

"It's your fault! It was you who went around telling your absurd lie, trying to show everyone that you are my savior and my father is a kidnapper! You, more than anyone else, know that it's not true. He saved my life. Or did you forget that you sold me and were going to sew me up for the wedding? You're not going to blackmail or manipulate me anymore like you used to. I'm no longer the girl who endured your torture without the right to scream or cry. Now I'm an adult, and will shout my truth wherever I go! Whether you like it or not, that's your problem, not mine."

"You've stepped into a dangerous situation, you brat, and you're going to pay for it!"

She hung up, leaving me on the other end of the phone, making me feel like I wasn't in my house anymore but in a dark and sinister forest, sensing that the ground beneath me was a huge pool of quicksand that was beginning to swallow and squeeze every muscle in my body. I couldn't move; I could barely breathe. Escaping from that relentless pit was not going to be easy. Despite it all, I was willing to fight and, if necessary, escape to wherever I needed to go.

By 2005, my father, my hero, had passed away, and I was left utterly alone. That same year, my mother's threats became constant. And when I went to see her in Chile, I made the big mistake of giving her my address and phone number. To her, I would be easy prey to trap.

And regarding the latter, I had no doubt whatsoever, for with her power, a mere snap of her fingers would be enough to make me vanish into thin air.

At that time, although Chile had returned to democracy and was governed under the presidency of Ricardo Lagos, Augusto Pinochet still lingered in the shadows, and he did so until 2006 when he passed away, surviving four years after that encounter with my grandfather Sergio Castillo at the Military Hospital, where all of this began. Chile transitioned to democracy, but deep down, the only thing that changed was that people no longer disappeared or were tortured, and tanks didn't roll through the streets. The country's major corporations and institutions were still led by high-ranking military officials who, of course, didn't wear uniforms but answered to a powerful group that would take many more years to disappear. It was a nation dressed in democracy, or rather, disguised.

In 1978, the CIA, the United States Central Intelligence Agency, concluded that the assassination of the Chilean ambassador in the United States, Orlando Letelier, under the presidency of Salvador Allende, was a "personal order" from Augusto Pinochet executed by an agent of the feared DINA (something like the German Gestapo but Pinochet-style).

That morning, the ambassador was driving his vehicle when, almost reaching the embassy building in Washington D.C., a bomb exploded from under his seat, taking his life and that of his colleague Ronny Moffitt in 1976. She was accompanied by her husband, who was sitting in the back seat and miraculously survived. Suppose the Chilean military power had been strong enough to assassinate an ambassador right under the nose and temple of American democracy. What would it cost my mother to pull a few strings and make me disappear from Hollister without anyone noticing my absence? All she had to do was claim to be a friend of the dictator and the daughter of the general who preceded him. My life was in danger, and once again, I had to forge a plan. My father wouldn't come to rescue me, nor would Monika, let alone the two Patricias, my aunt and the leech-like Sam. I had to figure things out on my own.

I thought about it for many nights, not just with one eye open and the other closed, but also unable to stop believing that I was once again fleeing from my mother's threats. I fueled my courage, gathered my strength, and avoided feeding fear, panic, dread, and paranoia as much as I could. But just in case, I had to do something. I mustered my courage, picked up the phone, and confronted her:

"Hello, Mom, how are you?"

"How do you think I am? You're going to regret what you've done! I'm going to come and kill you, you little shit!"

"Well, that's exactly why I'm calling you. I wanted to let you know that I'm leaving here soon and moving to Mexico, to Puerto Vallarta. I wanted to give you the news, so you don't waste your time looking for me here. Anyway, once I'm settled there, I'll let you know where I live in case you want to make amends with me and your soul."

We argued for a few minutes until I can't remember if she hung up abruptly or if I did. Nearly two months passed, and one day someone knocked on my door. I never received unexpected visitors at home, so I felt a chill down my spine, thinking that the door was a game of Russian roulette, and my seconds were numbered. It was the mailman. Usually, the man leaves the letters in the mailbox in front of the house and leaves. But this time, due to my mother's sinister intelligence, she arrived at my doorstep with a large yellow envelope stamped "certified". In order to receive the package, I had to sign a receipt that would be returned to the sender as proof of delivery. I stared into the mailman's eyes for a few seconds after realizing that the handwriting on the envelope was my mother's, and the return address was from Chile. But immediately, I made my terrified expression disappear and smiled at him, saying, "This person no longer lives here. I'm sorry." And so, I refused to accept the letter.

If I had told my mother that I was moving to Mexico, why would she send me a letter? I thought. So, I did as Elvis' song goes, please "return to sender." The kind mailman put the envelope back into his bag, stood at attention, and saluted me with his hand on his cap. "Have a nice day." As if that wasn't enough, a military mailman. Could it be that my grandfather Sergio's spirit possessed the mailman for a moment and came to certify, at the request of his daughter, whether I was really here or not? The point is, I suspected that my mother wanted to verify my whereabouts to plan her next move. Crazy but cunning, I never had any doubt about that. I took all possible precautions, disappeared from the map, and stopped calling her.

The New Era

Back in those days, people didn't rely excessively on social media as they do today. However, the most famous nerds of Silicon Valley had already embarked on a wild race towards the new virtual era. Just an hour away from where I lived, Steve Jobs stepped into the forefront of technological innovation to go head-to-head with Bill Gates. To keep up with this Californian advancement, I purchased my first phone with a digital screen. It didn't take long for Mark Zuckerberg to unveil his university project and launch Facebook as the primary tool for public gossip. It sparked a wave of unforeseen phenomena. Everyone began reconnecting with long-lost childhood friends, schoolmates, neighbors, and relatives who had disappeared somewhere in the world. Couples met, parents and children reunited, and siblings found each other. Family photographs were shared, new friendships were formed, romances blossomed, and public opinions were expressed about this or that photo. Personalities, trends, and personal data became the gateway to social media."

I had experienced many of these and had other firsthand experiences, from meeting my grandfather Armstrong to reconnecting with my father and later with my mother, all without the aid of electronic devices. Therefore, I didn't attach much importance to downloading the latest application. But due to the pressure and the same curiosity that killed the unknown but famous cat, I ended up becoming a new user of this platform. Who would have thought? It took me twenty minutes to learn how things worked, and another ten to discover that my mother was already ahead of me in this new cyber world, having her own Facebook profile, which I secretly started to spy on. Suddenly, she sent me a friend request. I never responded. Meanwhile, my mother was making an effort to quit drinking and regain control of her life.

By 2013, she had brought her cargo of cultural artifacts from Africa and in 2014, she opened her museum-exhibition for the first time in Chile at the Las Condes Cultural Center, an event called "Pequeños Grandes Poderes" (Little Great Powers) - Ancient African Goldsmithing. The catalog presented the following:

"The current exhibition consists of a collection of original pieces rescued and collected by Chilean anthropologist María Eugenia Castillo García-Huidobro, who has dedicated many years of her life to researching the cultures and civilizations of both Black Africa and Arab Africa (Berber). In this relentless pursuit and through her work, she has managed to compile nearly two thousand original pieces of great antiquity, highlighting among them the collection of metallurgies, of which a small part is being exhibited on this occasion. The exhibition consists of a collection of solid silver bracelets and earrings from Senegal, used by the Wolof and Pehul ethnic groups; some Berber jewelry pieces, mainly female adornments used in rituals and festivities such as marriages and funerals; and finally, we can be enchanted by the lost-wax bronze figures from the ancient Kingdom of (currently Benin), which delicately and gracefully show us the trades and daily activities of this social group."

The exhibition was a success and brought together the people Eugenia wanted to see. She reunited with the social class to which she belonged before venturing into the world, feeling at home, relieved, fulfilled, and happy. Her name, her surname, and her persona once again regained the importance they deserved in the cultural and social world of the Great Capital. In 2015, María Eugenia took advantage of the momentum and presented her second exhibition, "África Mágica" (Magical Africa), to the Santiago community:

"The exhibition is an invitation to immerse oneself in the culture of North Africa, where the sacred, the profane, and the decorative merge to reflect a worldview intimately linked to the magical world." Casa de lo Matta. Free admission.

Eugenia reached the pinnacle of success. Her guests praised her work, and she, personally, attended to the curiosity of journalists, authorities, educators, military personnel, ecclesiastics, and the general public. However, only a few members of my mother's family were present. As the days went by, Eugenia began to suffer once again from the abandonment and loneliness of those who initially believed all her lies. The house became too big for her, and despite Guillermina still keeping her company, the emptiness, memories, and ghosts of Sergio, her mother, and her past convinced her to put the property up for rent and move to her recently vacated apartment in Providencia. Since then, Guillermina returned to her own home but would come to take care of Eugenia occasionally, although she stayed more often than she left.

With clear symptoms of depression, among many other personality disorders, some time ago María Eugenia had joined a spiritual group in search of new friendships and experiences. There, my mother sought to definitively rid herself of her lifelong burdens. She wanted to find a path to her own salvation, liberate herself from her guilt, experience true repentance for the first time, take responsibility for her mistakes, and let all of that guide her toward the liberation of her ego and pride. Then she could gather strength, forgive herself, and eventually seek my forgiveness. There, she was an unknown, with no direct connections for anyone to judge her. Her intention was pure and sincere; she simply wanted to cleanse her heart of the guilt that prevented her from beating peacefully. There, she met the person who would become her new temporary friend and confidante, María Francisca Dolores Boisier Troncoso, both within and outside the spiritual group.

Through the Messenger platform, in this new era of sophistication, Eugenia began to inundate me with messages. This time, her tone was different. She subtly started to apologize for the "difficult times" and light veils of that nature. Then she became more sincere. I only read her messages but was afraid to respond. One day, I gathered the courage and sent her a link to a YouTube video about female genital mutilation in African girls. I asked her why she did that to me, why she caused me so much pain and imposed a trauma and a mark that would last a lifetime. She didn't respond or write to me anymore.

During those days, María Eugenia went away for a weekend to Viña del Mar to meet up with some of her friends, and when she returned to Santiago, perhaps due to sleepiness or having had a few drinks too many, she briefly closed her eyes on the road and veered onto the shoulder, colliding her car and leaving it wrecked. She was rushed to the emergency room, and they managed to save her life by swapping bones in her hips and legs for metal rods and treating the various bruises. Covered in bandages, she now resembled more of Cleopatra's mummy, and her condition was so deplorable that she not only needed continuous assistance but also a long list of medications to alleviate her new ailments that added to the previous ones. María Francisca then began to visit her to help with her medications, food, and chores in her apartment, trying to displace Guillermina from her duties. Soon enough, she gained my mother's trust and was even made responsible for managing her checkbook and paying various bills. My mother's condition didn't improve, and due to the abuses of her past life, her body appeared more and more exhausted. Her mind started to wander into the depths of her history; it became a habit and routine for her to visit the demons of her past that never left her in peace. The medications were insufficient, nothing eased her pain or remedied her growing schizophrenia.

She started writing to me on some occasions, until one day, in her right mind and with her heart in her hand, she apologized and finally acknowledged my own pain.

Eugenia wanted to shout to the world that she had released her dragons, but the dragons were old and had no intention of setting her free. She took a notebook and began writing down her ordeal with imprecise, meandering, obtuse handwriting, her mind making its best efforts to maintain control over herself during her days in bed. After a few months, she summoned strength from within and was able to stand, at least. The drugs and María Francisca's strange volunteer vocation were her best allies. And Guillermina, of course, as always, silently observing without saying anything.

(The following maintains a disorder of uppercase and lowercase letters and coherence, in an attempt to mimic, in some way, their confusing real manuscripts that I still possess)

"I write this on Monday, September 16. 1 Quetiapine 25 mg. ½ Dormonid Midazolam 1 Alprazolam 4 am: ½ Dormonid and 1 Alprazolam Night without deep sleep and NO rest. I wake up PHYSICALLY and INTELLECTUALLY EXHAUSTED. STRONG AND BELLIGERENT AGGRESSION - I FIGHT WITH MY 83-YEAR-OLD NANNY ALL DAY and I call her old, crazy, senile, useless, and other things. SHE PACKS HER BAG TO LEAVE! I take her out to eat in public to try to make things right, and I cry in public. INSUFFICIENT BENZODIAZEPINES + INSUFFICIENT REST.

Tuesday, September 17. DISASTER! Without Quetiapine, BY MISTAKE, I took a REFLEXAN in the middle of the night plus Benzodiazepines - a very ugly crisis upon waking up, with complete paralysis of BODY AND MIND. Unable to speak or move arms or legs.

Complete inability to speak or think. I called for HELP by phone, sending a written message to my ASSISTANT Karla Vargas, who came running in her car and brought me a giant empanada made by her grandmother...! And she made me eat it all, like a child! And she gave me a lot of tea she prepared (from leaves) to HYDRATE ME, FORCING me like a child since I didn't understand ANYTHING that was happening to me..."

Some time passed, and my mother dared to go out on the street. In line with her usual status and consistent with her lineage, she wore her gold locket around her neck, the same one she wore when she welcomed me at the airport on my first trip to Chile. This immediately caught the attention of some assailants who not only snatched the chain and her locket but also, due to her resistance, kicked her to the ground, breaking one of the metal rods keeping her arm in one piece. From that day on, my mother spiraled downhill, and her delusions and pains were unimaginable. Her routine was to stay awake all night, delirious and slaying demons, "dreaming of snakes" like Silvio Rodríguez song, alongside a large collection of pills. She would fall asleep around eight in the morning and wake up around 1 in the afternoon when she would have her coffee. For a few hours, María Eugenia managed to be lucid and realize that she was still alive. In those moments of clarity, she began to tell Guillermina and María Francisca about her intentions. She wanted to end her life. She couldn't bear her loneliness, her pains, the internal penance was unbearable.

"Guillermina, I can't take it anymore. I can't endure another day. Try to locate my daughter and tell her to forgive me, please. Tell her to come as soon as possible, I need to see her and give her something very important."

That afternoon, on July 28, 2015, Guillermina, as usual, brought the coffee to Eugenia's room around one-thirty. She approached the bed and tickled her feet to wake her up. My mother had some slight movements and reflexive responses. The elderly woman left the coffee on the nightstand and went around to the other side of the bed to adjust her pillow, only to discover a large number of empty medicine boxes and bottles, a broken glass, and Eugenia's scattered notes on the floor. Guillermina panicked and tried her best to wake up my mother. She picked up the phone and called María Francisca to ask for advice.

"Hello, hello, Miss Francisca, my boss is very ill, she doesn't want to wake up. I touch her feet and hands, and she reacts, but she doesn't wake up. Please come and help me, I don't know what to do!"

"Don't do anything, Guillermina. Let her sleep. Don't call anyone else and leave her in her room. I will come later. Don't worry and do as I say. Let her rest and close the door."

María Francisca had quickly become aware of my mother's fortune and made great efforts to gain her trust. Guillermina was merely a thorn in her side, easy to remove, and this was the moment she had been waiting for. For anyone in that situation, the most practical advice for a panicked elderly woman would have been to hang up and immediately call the paramedics. María Francisca had devised a whole plan, waiting for this precise moment without anyone noticing, not even Guillermina. Half an hour later, my mother breathed her last breath.

Soledad, a distant cousin whom I had the opportunity to meet during my trip to Chile, called the cousins in Brazil, daughters of my Aunt Patricia, to give them the news of my mother's passing. One of them immediately contacted me through social media to inform me of the sad news. María Francisca, in some way, had everything ready and prepared for when this would happen, so on that same day, they took my mother's lifeless body and organized a quick funeral. At that wake, where family and acquaintances began to arrive, Soledad, my mother's niece, delivered a few words of farewell and unexpectedly announced to everyone present that I had already been informed of what had happened and was on my way from the United States. When Soledad told everyone that I would soon be there to bid farewell to my mother, she, Guillermina, and several others saw in that woman's eyes the malice and intentions she carried with her. They also noticed the expression of concern and surprise that inevitably appeared on her face. The next day, María Francisca quickly organized the cremation of the body, without any investigation or autopsy to determine the cause of her death, all while I was buying plane tickets and finally accepting my mother's friend request on Facebook. On the fifth day, I set foot on Chilean soil for the second time. At the airport, this close friend of my mother, whom I met for the first time, came to pick me up and showed complete normality with my arrival without paying much attention to what had happened. She drove me to a hotel in the city that she had already booked.

"Andrea, I'll let you rest in this hotel, and we'll see each other tomorrow, okay?"

"No, ma'am, take me to my mother's house. I won't stay in a hotel."

"But you need rest, Andrea. Tomorrow, I'll come to pick you up. Does that sound good?"

"No, I insist, let's go to my mother's house, please."

When I entered Eugenia's house, the first thing that caught my attention was that the crystal chandelier from the dining room and other luxurious lamps that I had seen during my previous visit were missing. Only the cables were hanging from the ceiling. They had taken almost half of my mother's belongings. If I had stayed at the hotel, the house would have remained empty for the next morning. It had been a blatant, cruel, and cowardly looting. María Francisca wasted no time in getting rid of the possessions of the Castillo García-Huidobro family, knowing that I was the universal heir to everything. She made the documents my mother insisted I review disappear and swiftly obtained legal possession of all the properties with a lawyer by her side. She withdrew funds from bank accounts and made invaluable African collections and treasures that my mother left behind vanish, many of them part of her exhibitions and museums, pieces that had accompanied my childhood for many years. She didn't even give Guillermina a keepsake; instead, she dismissed her on the spot and sent her home to "retire". The audacious woman even dared to invite some friends from her "spiritual" group to come and take things from María Eugenia's house.

Poor Guillermina. She witnessed the deaths of Sergio, Teresa, and the two daughters she had raised since birth, Patricia and now Eugenia. What must she have thought of this rat who wanted to take even the memories?

I stayed at my mother's house that night. The walls were cold, and the shadows of the trees, illuminated by the streetlights, glided and caressed them, trailing along the floor. I sat on the bed for an indefinite period, feeling the same sensation as being in my room in Senegal, and instead of that intrusive shadow, I seemed to see the indelible bloodstain on the floor. At times, I held my breath to hear nothing and convinced myself that I was back while María Eugenia was gone and she couldn't harm me anymore. As the night wore on, the weight of the past pressed heavily on my mind. Memories flooded back, intertwining with the present moment. I could almost hear the echoes of whispered conversations and feel the palpable tension that once filled these walls. But amidst the nostalgia, a surge of determination rose within me. I refused to let the haunting presence of María Eugenia consume me any longer.

I was very confused and exhausted from the time difference between California and Santiago, Chile. I don't know at what hour I managed to fall asleep, but I'm sure that if I did, it was no more than an hour or two. It was a long night.

The next morning, I woke up to the chirping of birds in the garden, endlessly arguing, and then to the sound of a man knocking on the door, claiming to be an "appraiser" and needing to enter the house to do his work and assess whatever he found. I denied him entry and asked him not to come back. Immediately, I changed the lock on the door. My mother's thief never showed up again, seeing her plans frustrated. But not giving up, she sent a lawyer with the smell of alcohol and a worn collar who began pounding on the door. The guy recited a string of legal articles and adorned his proposal, using words I didn't understand, stating that I should immediately abandon the property but that they would be "very generous with me," offering me $40,000 in cash to return to the United States. Of course, I told him no and advised him to go and perform acts of charity alongside the appraiser. Soledad immediately helped me find a lawyer who told me that as the only daughter of María Eugenia, everything belonged to me according to Chilean law. My confusion was immense, but after fending for myself in life, I had little naivety left and realized that there were many hidden agendas here, and they had conspired to seize everything my mother left behind, including the museum. Unfortunately, I felt lost, disoriented, and powerless in the face of the corrupt pressure coming from all directions. My lack of knowledge in legal matters in the Spanish language overwhelmed me. Everyone wanted their piece of the pie, and they wanted it now. I asked my cousin Soledad to initiate the necessary legal proceedings while I returned to California to reorganize everything for whatever was to come. She did what she could to keep the vultures at bay, but at the same time, facing her own problems, she couldn't prevent the multilateral attack orchestrated by María Francisca Dolores Boisier.

In just a couple of months, at an extraordinary speed compared to the usual time it takes for legal processes in Chile, María Francisca took possession of everything and, as required by law, made a small publication in the official newspaper, which I didn't learn about until many years later:

"On December 14, 2015, in case number XYZX, the 23rd Civil Court of Santiago granted the effective possession of the estate inheritance left upon the death of Ms. María Eugenia Castillo García-Huidobro, which occurred on July 28, 2015, to Ms. María Francisca Dolores Boisier Troncoso, as the universal heir, without prejudice to the other legacies indicated in the open will granted on April 20, 2011, at the 51st Notary Public of Santiago by Mr. Iván Tamargo Barros. Secretariat 29-30-31."

I didn't know for certain how María Francisca managed to obtain a will from my mother. Whether she forged it and legalized it with the help of powerful influences interested in dividing the spoils, or simply took advantage of one of Eugenia's moments of madness and delirium that she was well aware of. Guillermina told me that she did her best to find that certified envelope that my mother sent me, and I refused to sign it out of fear that she would retaliate for daring to debunk her stories. During that time, feeling depressed, lonely, and mentally affected, Eugenia offered wills to all her friends in exchange for friendship. But the one in the envelope was meant for her only daughter and was made in her right mind when she realized that the idea of me going to Puerto Vallarta was a white lie. Perhaps unbeknownst to me, her will, more than an inheritance, was her way of saying "forgive me." What is certain is that when my mom received that envelope back, she wrote to me again, and I did receive that letter, which said:

Sept. 25, 2010.

My dear Andrea, beloved daughter,

Yesterday, October 6, was your birthday, and I wasn't in Santiago. I couldn't write or call you because I don't know your address or phone number to do so. Please, if you receive this letter, send me your new address in Mexico and your phone number. Also, your email address. I will be traveling to Senegal in December to sell my house there. My number is the same. It hasn't changed. Please, daughter, if you receive this letter, call or write to me immediately. I love you very much. Mom.

The dismantling of my mother's assets and everything she had inherited from my grandparents Sergio and Teresa Paulina was inevitable, corrupt, cruel, and completely disrespectful.

The amount I was able to salvage from the collections of jewelry, silverware, and African culture was very little. Those brief days at my mother's house were the first time I felt her presence, but this time the fear had dissipated, as it had vanished along with her existence.

With the help of Guillermina, I had the great fortune and luck to rescue perhaps the most valuable things that accompany me to this day and have become my daily therapy: the photos, documents, letters, and various notes that bring life and truth to my narrative. Without ever having discovered it, María Eugenia secretly kept the photos of my father, of their traveling and adventurous love, which I couldn't stop looking at over and over again. I found my childhood photos, among those dark-skinned people so different from me, and I relived the distant moments of my repressed childhood in Dakar, overwhelmed by pain and madness. I saw my father, my hero, sleeping in his bus in the middle of Paris or by the side of the road, barely covered with an old and worn-out towel. Through hundreds of letters, postcards, documents, and photographs, I uncovered the confusing corners of my life, gradually forging my own story. I realized that María Eugenia could never truly forget Samuel Armstrong, and for many years, she only made her best efforts to kill that love and unintentionally replace it with absurd hatred and revenge. My mother cherished their letters as her most precious treasure, along with the photographs from the day of my baptism to those showing the bruises on my face from the abuse. I continued to uncover her chest of memories, and my first tear was shed when I rediscovered Baba, my little white lamb. The second tear came when I saw Ruby.

As time passed, everything related to the Castillos García Huidobro vanished like the sun at sunset. Its main characters were also gone. The general was no longer there, my grandmother Paulina committed suicide, and my aunt Patricia and mother also took their own lives. My father was absent as well. In the end, only I remained, as lonely as when my mother disappeared in the African continent and didn't return for days.

Although this leech of a woman took everything, she couldn't prevent me from bringing half of my mother's ashes with me to the United States. The other half rests with her parents.

Redemption

South of San Francisco, passing through the Monterey Bay and the beautiful town of Carmel, begins a highway that winds along the cliffs, perpetually facing the Pacific Ocean. It is the Highway State Route 1, a road symbolized by sports convertibles cruising along California's favorite coastline, in spring adorned with yellow poppies everywhere. This is where this stretch begins, where it is impossible not to pull over and appreciate from above the immensity and cobalt blue of the ocean. If you're lucky, you might even spot California condors.

They call it "Big Sur", the big south. It was there that I took my mother's remains to rest in a beautiful and untouched place, like the border between the redwoods, the sea, and the sky. I opened the container with her ashes and watched as they mingled with the wind, in a moment as warm as those in Senegal...

"...This time, I am not running away from you, nor are you chasing me to hurt me. This time, we only meet again to avoid further suffering, and your African magic becomes real once more, creating a connection between your soul and mine, as I see you go with this wind, and I can see you smiling. It is difficult for me to hear your screams, and now I only feel your kiss. You no longer hate me, there is no more resentment. Finally, you have found peace by letting go of your demons to rescue me, to hold me in your arms again, drawing me close to your chest, protecting me. My heart is still broken, and it will take a long time to heal, but I promise you, Mom, now that I have accepted your forgiveness, I will tirelessly seek to reunite with you, with the best version of you. I will try to love you again as the mother who only existed in my dreams, and I know you will do the same to find me once more. Goodbye, Mom..."

I began traveling the world as my parents did. I returned to Senegal several times, meticulously exploring the streets, villages, and beaches of my childhood. My hand caressed the fishermen's boats, the nets, the sand, and even one of the walls of my old castle that was being partially demolished by its new owner. I saw dogs running through the streets and imagined seeing Ruby coming towards me, licking my wounds or joining me in tears. I found and embraced with all my strength my one and unforgettable friend, Alexandra. With her help and my limited resources, I founded a humble orphanage where a dozen children have a home, food, education, and love. I have wanted to legally adopt a little girl who stole my heart, and I haven't lost hope of making it a reality as soon as possible. However, the tragedy of COVID has halted and affected our way of life, limiting our ability to travel.

I rent a small house in Hollister and have been living modestly there for over 26 years, along with my cats, who are my family and confidants. Most of the day, I work as an assistant at an animal shelter where we receive abandoned, injured, and forgotten kittens and puppies daily. The shelter operates based on the constant flow of heartless individuals who see animals as disposable toys, devoid of feelings, intelligence, or emotions. On the other hand, some come to heal them, to adopt them, to volunteer, or to make a donation. It is a very challenging and sometimes thankless task the gratification comes from knowing that I have done the best I could for someone in need. When the evening comes, I go home, feed the rest of my family, my cats, take a shower, and then head out to take care of an elderly lady who also needs me. She reminds me of Guillermina. Sometimes, I stay with her throughout the night and return home at dawn. Whenever I have a few days off, I take the opportunity to go on hikes in the forests and parks of California, and each time I do so, I remember how my father enjoyed nature, the singing of birds, and the sound of streams and trees swaying in the wind.

Just like my mother, I have a passion for dance. During my time in high school, I developed a love for Arabic music and found myself swaying my hips to the beat of the drums, making the sequined hip scarf shimmer. However, my journey took a turn when I discovered salsa. Whenever there's a festival or party, I eagerly take to the dance floor, spinning and twirling with joy. Although, at this stage, my knee begs for a new kneecap, and I can only endure two or three songs before it demands respite. My favorite salsa band hails from Senegal, and they go by the name "Afrikando". Their infectious rhythms transport me back to the vibrant streets of my homeland, filling me with nostalgia and a renewed sense of pride.

Dance, for me, is not just a form of self-expression but a connection to my roots and a celebration of life's rhythm. Through movement, I find solace, joy, and a connection to the vibrant spirit of Africa.

My life has taken unexpected turns, filled with pain, loss, and the search for redemption. But amidst it all, I have found solace in the simple acts of kindness, in nurturing and caring for those who need it most. The wounds of the past may still linger, but I continue to move forward, embracing the beauty and resilience of life. And as I dance under the moonlight, I feel the presence of my parents, guiding me, and reminding me that redemption is possible, even in the face of darkness.

I don't have grand ambitions. I wish I had the knowledge to understand how Chilean legality works and find someone who can help me recover everything that belongs to my family without encountering corrupt people or opportunistic leeches. I don't intend to do anything petty or get involved in absurd greed. I just want to reclaim what is rightfully mine and belonged to my mother, by law, ethics, and morality. I know that in the Chilean community, I will find someone who will lend me a hand to achieve this. Through that endeavor, I can give back to Africa, reviving my mother's work to showcase the best of her and the beauty of the land where I was born. I also want to travel and have the means to support my orphanage and, if possible, create an animal sanctuary. That's all I want and long for.

Furthermore, I have decided to be happy and overcome my fears and traumas without resorting to any drugs, alcohol, or tobacco. I am proud of that, and I know that wherever they are, Eugenia and Sam are also proud to see me independent, working, and doing good wherever I go, however I can. It has not been an easy task at all. It took me a long time to understand and accept that Eugenia was also a victim. Her mother, devoid of affection and concerned about high society and its prejudices, never protected her from her abusive father, nor did she provide her with an example of how to be a mother.

Guillermina was instrumental in helping me understand the roots of María Eugenia's existential problems and the hidden secrets that led her to lose her balance. My father also helped me discover who she was and why she became that way. After her death, I gradually found the pieces and started putting the puzzle together. Over time, I have been able to fulfill my promise and forgive her from the bottom of my heart. This determination has also been crucial in finding my own healing, my own redemption, and freeing myself from any hatred, rejection, and fear I may have once felt towards her.

One of her sections of writing, in her right mind, that I was able to find, says...

My dear daughter,

I couldn't reply to you earlier because I was very ill, and Guillermina as well, with a nasty flu-influenza virus. You ask me how I can tell you that I love you after having done such terrible things to you in your childhood.

I would like to tell you that if I had the experience, knowledge, and wisdom that I have today, with my age, this would certainly not have happened. During those moments in your childhood, I was a young mother, alone, without advice or support from anyone. You were my only family. And I didn't know much about life, nor did I have anyone to guide me.

Now that I have acquired wisdom and knowledge through the experience of my years, you are far away and deeply wounded in your little heart, to the point that you can't even believe that I love you and that you are the only thing I have in life.

My mother passed away, my father too in 2002, and my only sister, your aunt Patricia, committed suicide on December 31, 2012. As you can see, I am alone as my immediate family has all gone. So, it is true when I wrote to you and write to you, telling you that I love you and that you are the only thing I have in the world. I repeat, in your childhood, I did things that were not appropriate. I was too young to know, without any experience or support to act better.

Try to understand this, as it is the only truth of everything that happened. Sometimes I think, if you could be reborn today, with my current experience and wisdom, how things would be different! I love you very much. You are the only treasure and valuable thing I have in the world.

Your Mom

One More Time

Here I am once again arriving in Senegal, and from the edge of the airplane wing, I try to relive that moment when Eugenia and Samuel, cheek to cheek, fought for the view from the window when they first arrived in this land that saw me born. It so happens that my two adjacent seats are empty from France, and I turn my head every now and then to imagine that Eugenia and Samuel are with me. There is my giraffe bathing in the sea, my courtyard, my home. My heart tightens and expands in its attempt to control my emotions. I welcome myself and gradually, slowly, I stop being the gringa or the Chilean, and I start to effortlessly flow between the culture that runs through my blood. The first thing I did was rush to visit my children and my friend Alexandra. We laughed a lot, played, talked, and drew. They have grown up. We stayed up late eating delicious food and telling stories by the bonfire on the beach.

The next morning, I said goodbye to everyone for the rest of the day to wander freely and reconnect alone with this land and my own history.

I picked the shortest beach that Sam and Eugenia had ever chosen. As I walk, my toes sink into the sand, and with each step, accompanied by my calm and deep breath and my gaze toward the horizon, I squeeze the memories and suppress the inevitable urge to cry. I don't want this breeze to dry my tears; I just want to let them go with the foam, as a tribute, as a gift, a thanksgiving to life.

Because despite all my ordeal, I discovered that life is beautiful and that pain is an essential part of it, so that we can appreciate happiness. Through fear, we can value the feeling of being safe, comfortable, and at ease. The universe functions in that way, everything possesses a negative and a positive pole, and magically, a flow is forged between the two, effortlessly.

We continue to develop experiences and absorb knowledge, some to become better, others worse. I have chosen to become better and let myself be carried away by the positive flow of the universe. I am free, no longer confined by walls that bounce back my sorrows. On the contrary, I am grateful that I can shout with happiness towards the sky and not expect an echo, a prohibition, or rejection. Similarly, I can smile or give without expecting anything in return. I am fully aware that my life may not be conventional and that the barriers I have had to overcome may surpass someone's imagination. But it is the reality I was destined to live, and while there are chapters I wouldn't want to repeat, I also find beautiful things within them.

Like the blind and stubborn sacrifice of a father, the complete selflessness of an animal's love, the smile of a stranger, the unconditional love of a friend, the remorse and sincere forgiveness of an executioner. I have learned that skin color doesn't matter, the color of the land doesn't matter, whether you're up or down, rich or poor, the flag or the nation doesn't matter. We all share the same desires, needs, and fears. We all walk in the same direction, with varying degrees of effort, in search of learning and the imperfect notion of happiness. The mere miracle of existing on this unique and special planet, surrounded by other universes and galaxies that perhaps envy and curiosity gaze upon us, is reason enough to consider it an obligation to take a minute in life to pause and observe everything in silence, as I am doing now, on this beach...

A seagull flies overhead. The breeze caresses my face and hair like a mother's hand overflowing with love. I feel more alive than ever, realizing that there are only a few things we need to be happy, we just have to pay attention. A fisherman in the distance greets me, and I tilt my hat to reciprocate his friendship. The salty foam heals me once again, soothing my last wounds, cleansing me, and the sun blesses me, while a small crab near my foot watches me as if wanting to say, "This rock is mine."

I know it's yours, my dear friend. I know it's your home. Would you let me stay for one more minute? Nice to meet you, Mr. Crab.

My name is Fabi, the daughter of Ifa, the Daughter of Africa, and I have returned to be happy.

THE END

Rectangular Memories

María Eugenia, Sergio Castillo and Augusto Pinochet

My grandparents Teresa and Sergio with President Frei Montalva

Sergio Castillo (at center) at Independence Day Parade

Sergio and Eugenia

María Eugenia and Sergio Castillo

Sergio Castillo with President Salvador Allende

Mom and Dad , very young

The traveling bus of Sam and Eugenia

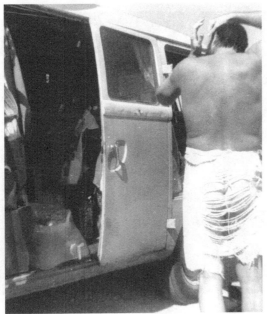

My father after a shower, somewhere in Europe

Awakening on a Street in France (picture taken by María Eugenia)

María Eugenia posing for Sam lens

Eugenia and Sam at my baptism party

Samuel in Casablanca, Morocco

My first months with Sam and Eugenia

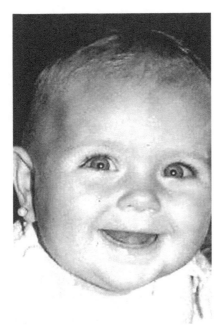

My first years

Mamina and Eugenia carring me in kanga

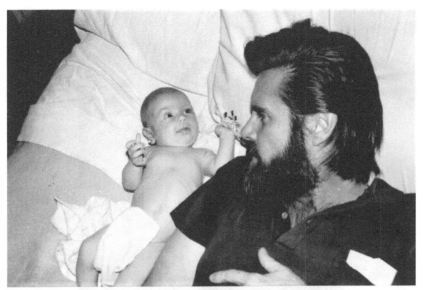

My first month with dad and mom

Crist Santosol

Baba and me growing together.

With Samuel

Playing with Ruby. Below with my eye healing and some friends

Last days of Sam in Dakar

The bugs of Sam and Eugenia

María Eugenia dressed as locals

My mother dancing

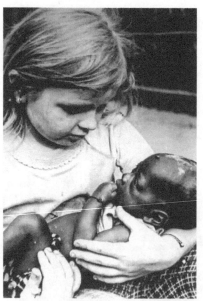

Me taking care of a baby

My mother working on IFAN

Eugenia with President of Senegal Leopold Senghor

Her first rituals

Eugenia y sus amigos

Friends of my mother

The Daughter of Africa

The religious clases

Harvesting fruits on the castle

"The castle of the Castillo's"

Newspaper notices of my disappearance.

My grandparents visiting

Eugenia

"Kenny Rogers"

Little time before escape with Sam

With Melanie y Katie en Hollister

María Eugenia father's farewell speech

Funeral of Sergio Castillo - Escuela Militar, Santiago of Chile

With my kids in Senegal

About The Author

Crist Santosol, an independent literary author of Chilean nationality, is distinguished for weaving stories based on the complexities of human experiences and relationships, with a simple and light approach that nuances the plot in a constructive, realistic, and easily digestible manner.

In his works, such as "La Hija de África," "La Palma de Mi Mano," "Amadeus TZ45," "El Ultimo Selk'nam," "Kundi," " Una Historia de Color Azul" and others, Santosol manages to expose the best values of his characters in a captivating, familiar, and enjoyable way.

Santosol does not limit himself to the literary field alone but also stands out as a musician and multidisciplinary artist. Like his narratives, in his artistic expressions, he seeks to elevate the best of humanity and society, carrying a profound message that evokes planetary care, ecological awareness, and animal compassion.

Santosol's cultural vision is broad and diverse, shaped by his own life and worldview. Through his art, he not only entertains but also invites reflection on the importance of fundamental values and connection with our environment. With a committed gaze, Crist Santosol leaves a mark that extends beyond the pages of his books, embracing social and environmental responsibility in his artistic expression.

Thank you for reaching this far.

Contact: Cristsantosolcontact@gmail.com

Made in United States
Cleveland, OH
27 January 2025